QUESTIONS IN HISTORY

Series editor: Alan White

LENIN'S RUSSIA

Alan White

D1424143

Collins Educational

Published by Collins Educational
An imprint of HarperCollins*Publishers*
77–85 Fulham Palace Road
London W6 8JB

First published 1998, reprinted 1998

ISBN 0 00 327119 6

**British Library Cataloguing in
Publication Data**
A catalogue record for this book is available
from the British Library.

Acknowledgements

The author and publishers would like to thank
the following for permission to reproduce
illustrations:

David King Collection (pp35, 40).

**Cover photograph: David King
Collection.**

Edited by Lucy Courtenay
Series design by Derek Lee
Map drawn by Raymond Turvey
Picture research by Lucy Courtenay
Production by Sue Cashin

Printed and bound by Scotprint Ltd,
Musselburgh

Contents

1 Introduction

Lenin before 1917

Lenin was born Vladimir Ilyich Ulyanov at Simbirsk (now Ulyanovsk), four hundred miles to the east of Moscow, in April 1870. His family background was, in late 19th-century Russian terms, a highly privileged one. His father was a school inspector with a rank in the Tsarist civil service equivalent to that of a major-general in the army, and his mother was the daughter of a doctor and landowner. The young Ulyanov excelled at school, and in 1891 – having been expelled from Kazan University in 1887 for taking part in a student demonstration – he took a first-class honours degree in law as an external student of St Petersburg University.

The first phase of Lenin's adult life was spent as a political exile, first in Siberia (1897–1900) and then in Western Europe (1900–1917), mostly in Switzerland. It was in his early years as an exile that Ulyanov became Lenin, a pseudonym derived from the name of the Siberian river Lena.

The second phase of Lenin's adult life opened in April 1917, when he returned to Russia following the collapse of Tsarism in the February Revolution. In October 1917, without any real administrative training or experience, he became Russia's head of government. There followed four and a half years of unremitting work which destroyed his health. Lenin suffered major strokes in May 1922 and March 1923 before dying in January 1924, aged only 53, as the result of a third stroke. During this final period he was incapable of sustained political activity.

Marxism

Lenin became a committed opponent of Tsarism while still in his teens. A formative influence upon him was the execution in 1887 of his older brother, Alexander Ulyanov, as a result of his involvement in a plot to assassinate Tsar Alexander III. Initially Lenin was attracted towards populism, the late 19th century opposition movement calling for the replacement of Tsarism with a uniquely Russian brand of peasant-oriented socialism, but in the early 1890s he became one of a growing number of Russian adherents of Marxism.

In some ways it is surprising that Marxism had an impact in late 19th-century Russia. It was not a doctrine with obvious relevance to Russian conditions. At the centre of Marxist thinking was the belief that in industrialised (or 'capitalist') societies the possessing class, the bourgeoisie, grew progressively richer and numerically smaller while the proletariat, people with nothing to sell but their own labour, grew poorer and numerically larger. This process eventually saw the proletariat reaching breaking point. The outcome was revolution followed by the creation of a classless communist society.

Marxist doctrine thus maintained that proletarian revolutions could only occur in mature industrial societies. Late 19th-century Russia, however, was very far from being a mature industrial society. In the 1890s over 80% of Russians were peasants engaged in subsistence farming.

Bolsheviks and Mensheviks

The first Marxist organisation to which Lenin belonged was the Union of Struggle for the Liberation of the Working Class, which he joined in St Petersburg in 1895. His involvement with the Union led first to his imprisonment in St Petersburg (1895–97) and then to exile in Siberia. During his Siberian exile he became associated with the All-Russian Social-Democratic Labour Party (RSDLP), which was founded in 1898. On his release from exile, Lenin opted to continue the revolutionary struggle from a base abroad. His first project in foreign exile was the production of an underground revolutionary newspaper, Iskra (The Spark) which was to be distributed covertly throughout Russia. The first issue of Iskra appeared in 1900.

In 1903 at its Second Congress, the infant RSDLP split. Ostensibly the dispute was about political tactics. Lenin wanted the RSDLP to become a party of elite professional revolutionaries operating under tight centralised leadership. His opponents, led by Yuli Martov (real name Tsederbaum), favoured a broader-based, more decentralised party in which rank-and-file working-class members would have a say in the making of policy.

However, behind this dispute over tactics, there were other more fundamental differences. Martov, an orthodox Marxist, believed that Russia's proletarian revolution was a long way off. In the short term, he wanted to see the country's industrial workers developing effective trade unions to defend their interests. Lenin and his followers, by contrast, were impatient for revolutionary action and saw trade union activity as an irrelevant distraction.

At the 1903 Congress, Martov was defeated by Lenin. His followers became known as Mensheviks (minority) while Lenin's became known as Bolsheviks (majority). At the time of the downfall of Tsarism in 1917, however, Mensheviks were more numerous in Russia than Bolsheviks.

Lenin's personality

Lenin believed that revolutionaries had to be rock hard. This attitude left little room for sentiment. Lenin had colleagues and followers rather than friends. Even his marriage to Nadezhda Krupskaya was a political partnership more than anything else. There were no children. 'As a private man', writes Orlando Figes (A People's Tragedy: The Russian Revolution 1891–1924, 1996), 'there was nothing much to Lenin: he gave himself entirely to politics.' In his political dealings, Lenin's attitude to subordinates who bungled things was in general ill-tempered and unforgiving, while those who crossed or challenged him were abused and reviled. 'Cretins', 'bloodsuckers', and 'scum' were among the more repeatable labels he applied to his political opponents.

Lenin's uncompromising and confrontational approach to politics reached its peak in the period of the Civil War, when he became an unapologetic advocate of political terror. The prevailing circumstances, he claimed, demanded 'iron discipline' and an 'iron party'. There was, however, something more to Lenin than fanaticism, intolerance and ruthlessness. He was entirely lacking in vanity. He was neither self-seeking nor corrupt. As Russia's head of government he lived modestly. Unlike Stalin (see p46, Key Reference), Hitler and Mussolini he remained a civilian, never becoming a uniform-wearing militarist. There was too, as Robert Service points out, a kind of idealism behind the obsession with brutal methods: 'His vision of a future for mankind when all exploitation and oppression would disappear was sincere' (*Lenin: A Political Life*, vol 3, 1995).

Lenin as a political theorist

Lenin was throughout his life a prolific writer on political and economic subjects. His collected works have been published in fifty-five volumes. However, estimates of Lenin's importance as a political theorist vary. After Lenin's death, the doctrines of the ruling Communist Party in the Soviet Union were officially described as Marxism-Leninism rather than plain Marxism – implying that Lenin's contribution to Communist doctrine was no less significant than that of Marx. 'By his writings', claimed a biography published by Moscow's Institute of Marxism-Leninism in 1965, 'Lenin enriched all the component parts of Marxism.' Western commentators have generally taken rather a different view. 'Lenin', says John Plamenatz (*German Marxism and Russian Communism*, 1954), 'was not a philosopher or social theorist of even secondary importance.'

What needs to be borne in mind, of course, is that Lenin did not see himself primarily as a philosopher or social theorist. Like Marx, his purpose was not so much to understand the world as it was to change it. Lenin's principal writings, notably *What Is To Be Done?* (1902), *Imperialism: the Highest Stage of Capitalism* (1916) and *The State and Revolution* (1917), were onslaughts on his political enemies. In *What Is To Be Done?* he made out the case for a leading party of professional revolutionaries, which he went on to deploy against Martov and others in the Social Democratic Congress of 1903. In *Imperialism* he tried to show that capitalism, far from being capable of delivering improvements in working-class living standards, as alleged by the German 'revisionist' socialist Edward Bernstein ('revisionist' because he sought to revise Marx's ideas), was in fact a decaying and bankrupt system on the verge of collapse. In *The State and Revolution* he sought to ridicule those on the political left in Russia in 1917 who favoured the introduction of a democratic constitution.

To the Finland Station, 1917

When Nicholas II abdicated in early March 1917, Lenin was living in Zurich. Naturally he was desperate to return to Russia so as to be in a position to influence events. However, getting back to Russia was not a simple matter. No help could be expected from Russia's wartime allies, Britain and France. Their fear was that once in Russia's capital, Petrograd (the wartime name for St Petersburg), Lenin would become a destabilising force in politics and would as a result undermine the Russian and Allied war efforts.

From the German point of view though, the prospect of Bolshevik-inspired destabilisation in Petrograd was an attractive one. In the spring of 1917 the German authorities made contact with Lenin through intermediaries. An agreement was reached to allow Lenin to cross Germany in a sealed train, which was swiftly arranged. Having crossed Germany, Lenin travelled through neutral Sweden and Finland before arriving at Petrograd's Finland Station on 3 April. In Petrograd the circumstances surrounding Lenin's return to Russia were a matter of public knowledge, and gave rise to persistent accusations in 1917 that he was a German agent.

2 *The October Revolution*

Popular uprising or a Bolshevik coup d'etat?

Key points

◆ After the collapse of Tsarism there was a breakdown of authority
◆ The Bolsheviks, insignificant in February 1917, increased their support through Lenin's April Theses
◆ The Bolsheviks lost political ground in the July Days but the Kornilov affair enabled them to recover
◆ The Bolsheviks had extensive support in Petrograd at the time of the October Revolution but not the support of the Russian majority
◆ Without Lenin the Bolsheviks would not have won control in 1917

The political setting

The collapse of Tsarism

The downfall of Tsarism in 1917 was welcomed by all classes in Russia:

◆ Middle-class liberals, frustrated before 1914 by the absence of a genuine constitution, were incensed during the war years by Tsarist mismanagement of the Russian war effort.

◆ The peasantry, a volatile class before the war due to poverty and land hunger, were by 1917 (in the words of the novelist Bunin) 'growing more furious every day'. This was largely the result of the impact of conscription. Between 1914 and 1917, 14 million men were conscripted into the Russian army, the vast majority of them peasants. Nearly 2 million were killed in action and 8 million were either wounded or taken prisoner.

◆ The urban working classes, disaffected before 1914 by appalling living and working conditions, were further embittered during the war by inflation and food shortages. Their mass demonstrations in Petrograd because of food shortages and the subsequent mutiny of the Petrograd garrison, known collectively as the February Revolution, resulted in Nicholas II losing control of his capital city. He abdicated soon afterwards (2 March 1917).

The February Revolution was a spontaneous affair. The demonstrators were not controlled or manipulated by political leaders. For the most part, opposition politicians were caught off balance by the events of February 1917. As a result there was no ready-made government waiting to take over when the Tsar abdicated. Into this political vacuum moved two bodies: the Provisional Government and the Petrograd soviet.

The Provisional Government

The Provisional Government, formed in early March 1917, consisted largely of members of the Constitutional Democratic (or Cadet) and Octobrist parties. There was also a sprinkling of independents. The Cadets and the Octobrists, more right-wing than the Cadets, were liberal parties. Their main aims were:

◆ to equip Russia with a constitution that would end Tsarist autocracy.

◆ to establish a law-making body with meaningful powers.

◆ to guarantee basic rights such as freedom of speech.

Support for the Cadets and Octobrists was effectively confined to Russia's diminutive urban middle class.

The Provisional Government's prime minister was Prince Lvov, a well-meaning but ineffectual landowner with extensive experience in local government. However, Lvov was head of the government in name only. The dominant figure in the Provisional Government was its Foreign Minister, the hard-working but unimaginative Cadet leader P.N. Milyukov. Also influential was the industrialist Alexander Guchkov, leader of the Octobrists, who held the post of Minister of War and the Navy.

The Provisional Government was a self-appointed body, not an elected one. Its claim to rule rested solely on the fact that its members had been leading figures in the Duma, the largely powerless elected assembly which had been established during the 1905 revolution. There was, however, no expectation that the Provisional Government would govern for long. It was generally accepted that its role was to be a caretaker government, administering the country's affairs while preparations were made for elections to a Constituent Assembly, whose function would be to draw up a democratic constitution for Russia.

The Petrograd soviet

The Petrograd soviet was a revival of the St Petersburg soviet, or council of workers, which had been set up during the 1905 revolution. The difference between the 1917 soviet and its predecessor was that it contained representatives of Petrograd's army garrison as well as of its factory workers.

The Petrograd soviet had 3,000 members. There was a representative from each battalion (250 men) of the Petrograd garrison and one representative for every 1,000 factory workers. How long each member served was a matter for the army unit or factory he represented. The composition of the soviet could therefore change quite abruptly. In early 1917 it was dominated by Mensheviks and Socialist Revolutionaries, but later in the year their influence waned.

The Socialist Revolutionaries (SRs) were the party of the peasantry. They wanted Russia to remain a largely agricultural country in which land was owned and farmed on a communal rather than a private basis. They were also suspicious of strong central government, and wanted localities to have as much control over their own affairs as possible. The principal architect of these plans for peasant-based socialism was Victor Chernov (1873–1952). The SRs' main weakness as a party was their internal disunity.

Soviets sprang up all over Russia in 1917. By October, there were around 900 of them. The Petrograd soviet, however, was far more important than any of the others. In 1917, Petrograd was the cockpit of the revolution. What happened in Petrograd shaped events elsewhere, not the other way round.

Relations between the Provisional Government and the Petrograd soviet

After the February Revolution, the Provisional Government needed the approval of the Petrograd soviet in order to function. The soviet had the allegiance of Petrograd's garrison, and by virtue of support from railway and postal workers it controlled Petrograd's links with the outside world. The Provisional Government, by contrast, had no real power at its disposal. 'The Provisional Government', wrote Guchkov in March 1917, 'exists only as long as it is allowed to do so by the soviet.'

The Menshevik and SR leaders who dominated the Petrograd soviet could have set themselves up as Russia's caretaker government after the February Revolution. They chose not to do so. Instead they opted for a watchdog role. Middle-class liberal politicians were to administer the country's affairs while the Petrograd soviet kept their activities under review, threatening to intervene in the event of any departure from revolutionary principles. Lenin called this arrangement 'dual power'.

There were a number of reasons, ideological and practical, why the Mensheviks and SRs were unwilling to take control in March 1917:

◆ The Mensheviks were orthodox Marxists. In developing capitalist countries such as Russia, according to Marx, the dominant class was the bourgeoisie, the industrial working class being too weak to challenge its power. In these circumstances, the Mensheviks believed there was no alternative to allowing the 'bourgeois' politicians – Milyukov and his followers – to lead the way. SR leaders, though not Marxists, were strongly influenced by Menshevik thinking.

◆ Conscious of their lack of administrative experience, Mensheviks and SRs believed themselves to be unqualified to govern.

◆ There was a fear that Russia's conservative army commanders might try to overthrow a socialist government, plunging the country into civil war.

The April Crisis

The Menshevik and SR abstention from power did not last long. In April–May 1917, the Petrograd soviet and the Provisional Government collided on the issue of war aims.

In the First World War, the Cadets and Octobrists wanted to fight Germany and Austria until a decisive victory had been won. The Mensheviks and the SRs, on the other hand, were altogether more lukewarm in their attitude to the war. They favoured fighting a defensive war while persuading the other combatants to agree to a peace settlement 'without annexations and indemnities' – that is, without gains or losses of territory and without payments by the defeated to the victors. This policy of 'revolutionary defensism' was set out in the Petrograd soviet's 'Appeal to All the Peoples of the World' (March 1917).

In April it became known in Petrograd that Milyukov had sent Russia's allies a diplomatic note distancing himself from 'revolutionary defensism'. Uproar followed. Demonstrators filled the streets. Guchkov resigned. Milyukov was forced to follow suit (4 May). The Provisional Government was reconstructed, and now included Irakli Tsereteli, the ablest of the Mensheviks, and the SR leader Victor Chernov, amongst others. Some Cadets remained in the government in minor posts, but in spring 1917 Russia's liberals were effectively consigned to what

Trotsky (see p46, Key Reference) called 'the dustbin of history'. It was during the early stages of this April Crisis that Lenin arrived back in Russia.

Alexander Kerensky

The dominant figure in the reconstructed Provisional Government was not Tsereteli or Chernov but the 36-year-old SR lawyer Alexander Kerensky. Ambitious, impulsive and eloquent, Kerensky was the Provisional Government's Minister of Justice between March and May 1917. He owed his appointment to Milyukov, who, aware of Kerensky's popularity among Petrograd's factory workers, thought he would be a useful intermediary between the Government and the Petrograd soviet. Following the April Crisis Kerensky took over Guchkov's post as Minister of War and the Navy. He became prime minister when Prince Lvov resigned in July, and held this post until ousted from it by the October Revolution. After 1918 Kerensky lived in exile in France and the United States, dying in 1970 at the age of 89.

Lenin's April Theses

Bolshevik divisions

Bolshevik political activity in Petrograd in 1917 got under way while Lenin was still in exile. Command was assumed by a three-man committee headed by L.B. Kamenev (see p46, Key Reference), one of the most senior figures in the Bolshevik hierarchy. One of the other members of the committee was the 38-year-old Josef Djugashvili, better known as Stalin.

Kamenev's analysis of the situation in Russia at this point was virtually identical to that of the Mensheviks. He believed that the country was experiencing a 'bourgeois revolution', and that the proletarian revolution envisaged by Marx was still a long way off. He therefore adopted a policy of support for the Provisional Government. He also argued for collaboration, possibly even a merger, with the Mensheviks. Stalin was in agreement with these views.

Lenin, though, rejected them completely. On his arrival in Russia, he insisted that the Bolsheviks should launch a bid for power within a matter of months. He called for outright opposition to the Provisional Government and dismissed the idea of collaboration with the Mensheviks. Kamenev and other Bolsheviks thought that Lenin had taken leave of his senses. Not only were they shocked by his apparent willingness to disregard Marxist theory – which implied that the progression from feudalism to capitalism and then on to communism would be a prolonged affair – but they also believed him to be seriously out of touch with the mood of the Russian people.

There followed a brief period of in-fighting within the Bolshevik ranks, which ended with Lenin getting his way. His success owed much to the force of his personality, but it also owed something to support from new entrants into the Bolshevik party. These new Bolsheviks, radical in outlook and mostly working-class in origin, preferred Lenin's audacity to Kamenev's caution.

At the time of the February Revolution, the Bolsheviks had 25,000 members in Russia. By April, this figure had risen to 75,000. Lenin knew this was an inadequate platform from which to launch a bid for power, and set out to attract more support. His chosen method was a series of policies designed to exploit the frustrations within the army, the peasantry and the industrial working class. Lenin published his programme in the form of a ten-point document, later known as the April Theses. At the heart of the April Theses were distinctive views on the future of the soviets, the land question and the issue of war and peace.

'All power to the soviets'

One point on which Octobrists, Cadets, Mensheviks and SRs were agreed was that Russia's political future should be decided by a democratically-elected Constituent Assembly. In the April Theses Lenin staked out a different position. His view was that the soviets should become the basis of government in post-revolutionary Russia. Lenin justified his opposition to a Constituent Assembly in terms of Marxist doctrine, claiming that a communist state could never be built on 'bourgeois democracy'. But his thinking was almost certainly influenced as much by tactical considerations as it was by abstract theory:

◆ The demand for soviet power was calculated to appeal to the workers and soldiers who elected the Petrograd soviet. The soviets faced an uncertain future once a Constituent Assembly was elected, as they would have no obvious purpose. Lenin's policy offered the prospect of continued power and influence for the soviets.

◆ Lenin knew that the Bolsheviks had no real chance of winning a majority in nation-wide free elections. However, the Petrograd and other soviets' rough-and-ready methods of election offered the Bolsheviks the opportunity of winning control within a relatively short space of time.

'All land to the peasantry'

The early 20th-century Russian peasantry was land hungry. Peasant land hunger had two main causes:

◆ The nature of the land settlement which accompanied the abolition of serfdom in 1861. Serfdom was a form of slavery under which peasants were legally the property of their masters. Before emancipation, serfs were given land to cultivate for subsistence purposes in return for the work they did on their owners' estates. In 1861 these allotments of land became peasant property. It was not an especially generous settlement, as only one-third of Russia's arable land was transferred to the peasantry. The other two-thirds remained in the hands of the state, the church and the nobility. In addition, the peasantry were made to pay for what they received, for the state bought out the landowners and re-sold land to villages in return for 49 annual 'redemption payments'.

◆ The population explosion which took place in late 19th-century Russia. In 1861 Russia's rural population numbered 70 million. By 1917 it was 130 million. In the half-century after 1861 villages were able to buy or rent some extra land, but for the most part not enough to meet their fast-growing needs. The money needed for rent or purchase was not available. Peasants tried to work their existing land harder, but there were limits to what could be achieved through more intensive cultivation. In these circumstances, peasants understandably looked enviously in the direction of the privately-owned estates in their localities.

In the months following the February Revolution, the idea took root among the peasantry that there would be no brutal government response to militancy in the countryside of the kind which had occurred after the 1905 revolution, when P.A. Stolypin, the Tsar's chief minister, had suppressed rural protest by hanging so many of its ringleaders that the noose had become known as 'Stolypin's necktie'. Believing themselves to be safe from reprisals, peasants began to seize control of landowners' estates by force.

The reconstructed Provisional Government, with Victor Chernov as Minister of Agriculture, was fully alive to the need for land reform. It refused, however, to sanction land seizures, insisting that land reform was a matter for the Constituent Assembly. The Provisional Government adopted this position for three main reasons:

◆ It wanted land reform to be carried out lawfully.

◆ It wanted land reform to be fair, rather than a disorderly scramble.

◆ It feared that going ahead with land reform while Russia was still at war could lead to wholesale desertions, with soldiers of peasant origin leaving the front for their home villages in order to get their share of land.

Unlike the Provisional Government, the Bolsheviks encouraged land seizures. Their policy was 'All land to the peasantry'. It was an opportunistic policy. The Bolsheviks gave the impression that they wanted landowners' estates to become the peasantry's private property, despite the fact that as socialists they were opposed to the principle of private landownership. It was, however, a policy which helped to win the Bolsheviks support in Petrograd. This was because the soldiers of the Petrograd garrison were mostly of peasant origin and because Petrograd factory workers often retained close links with their home villages. The impact of the policy outside Petrograd, where information might have been limited, is harder to calculate.

Peace

One of the strongest currents flowing through Russia in 1917 was the desire for peace. Anti-war feeling was especially strong in Petrograd, which had been badly hit by inflation. It was strong at the front line too. 'The soldiers wanted only one thing – peace, so that they could go home and rob the landowners', recalled Brusilov, commander-in-chief of Russia's armies in the spring of 1917, in his memoirs. In the heady days following the February Revolution, it appeared possible that the Menshevik–SR policy of 'revolutionary defensism' would quickly bring about the end to the war which was hoped for so fervently.

Subsequently though, it became clear that the other European powers were in no hurry to negotiate. It was in this context that Lenin called for a separate peace, negotiated directly with the Central Powers without the involvement of Russia's allies. By doing so, he aligned the Bolsheviks with the trend of opinion in Petrograd. He also did this with his policies on soviet power and the land issue. In contrast, the Provisional Government began to lose touch with public opinion (see p13, Figure 1).

The July Days

In mid-1917, an opportunity arose for Lenin to use the Bolsheviks' new-found

Figure 1
Summary of the policy differences between the Provisional Government and the Bolsheviks, spring–summer 1917

	Provisional Government	**Bolsheviks**
Constitution	A new constitution to be drawn up by a democratically-elected Constituent Assembly	A political system based on councils of workers' and soldiers' representatives (soviets)
Land issue	Land reform to be left to the Constituent Assembly: against illegal land seizures	Legitimisation of the peasant land seizures taking place in 1917
War and peace	Search for a negotiated general peace: defence of Russian territory in the meantime.	Unqualified opposition to the war: a separate peace to be made with the Central Powers

popularity in Petrograd to launch the bid for power that he had been contemplating since his arrival at the Finland Station. On 20 June, the Provisional Government ordered units of the Petrograd garrison to the war front. The units in question mutinied, claiming that they had a right to remain in Petrograd to defend the revolution against its enemies. Radical elements among Petrograd's factory workers rallied to their support. So too did the pro-Bolshevik sailors of the Baltic fleet, based at the island fortress of Kronstadt 20 miles off Petrograd in the Gulf of Finland. In early July, a large contingent of Kronstadters arrived in Petrograd to lend their weight to the embattled soldiers. Massive street demonstrations followed. All the elements for a successful Bolshevik insurrection now appeared to be in place.

Lenin called for further demonstrations. Then, at the crucial moment, he hesitated. He failed to give the crowds a clear lead. Kerensky's government counter-attacked. The mutinous soldiers were disarmed. *Pravda*, the Bolshevik newspaper, was suppressed. Warrants were issued for the arrest of Lenin and other leading Bolsheviks. Lenin fled to Finland, where he remained until shortly before the October Revolution.

The Kornilov affair

The July Days were a disaster for the Bolsheviks. Their organisation was broken. Their leaders were either imprisoned or forced into hiding. They appeared to have lost their opportunity to take power. At this point, however, they were blessed with a slice of good fortune. It came in the form of General Kornilov's intervention in politics.

Lavr Kornilov was a fighting general of limited political grasp. One of his fellow-officers said of him that he had 'the heart of a lion, the brain of a sheep'. After the February Revolution, Kornilov commanded the Petrograd garrison for two months before returning to the front in April. He watched events unfold in 1917 with mounting disgust. After the July Days he made no attempt to conceal his wish to restore order in Petrograd and discipline in the army. His reputation won him a significant following among the Petrograd middle class, and this in turn made him a figure of political consequence.

Kerensky, the undisputed head of the Provisional Government since the July Days, responded to Kornilov's ascent by promoting him to the post of commander-in-chief of Russia's armies, in place of Brusilov. Following his appointment, Kornilov demanded powers which would have effectively made him a military dictator. This led to a series of confused and inconclusive negotiations with Kerensky. When these negotiations broke down in August 1917, Kornilov ordered a detachment of his forces to advance on Petrograd.

Here, it appeared, was a counter-revolution in the making. The response of the Petrograd soviet was to mobilise its resources to defend the capital.

Bolsheviks were very much to the fore. Bolshevik Red Guards (armed factory workers) who had been disbanded after the July Days were re-armed. Pro-Bolshevik railwaymen held up troop trains heading towards Petrograd. Crucially, representatives of the Petrograd soviet, many of them Bolsheviks, infiltrated Kornilov's advancing forces and succeeded in turning the men against their officers. The advance on Petrograd petered out without a shot being fired.

The Kornilov affair had two main political consequences:

◆ The collapse of Kerensky's reputation. His dealings with Kornilov left him vulnerable to the charge that he had taken part in a counter-revolutionary plot.

◆ A sharp upswing in the Bolsheviks' popularity. They more than anyone, it appeared, had been responsible for the defeat of Kornilov.

In September the Bolsheviks won control of the Petrograd soviet and of the soviets in a number of other major cities, Moscow among them.

The October Revolution

In October 1917, Petrograd was effectively at the Bolsheviks' mercy. The main levers of power in the city were in their hands. These included the Military Revolutionary Committee (MRC) set up by the Petrograd soviet after the Kornilov affair to organise forces for use against counter-revolutionaries. The question of how best to exploit the opportunities which now presented themselves was debated at a crucial meeting of the party's Central Committee (see p32, Figure 5) on 10 October. Lenin made a flying visit to Petrograd in order to be present. He argued for an immediate seizure of power. Kamenev and Grigory Zinoviev (see p46, Key Reference) urged caution but they lost the argument. The Committee voted 10–2 in favour of an insurrection.

At the tactical level, the Bolshevik seizure of power was planned and directed not by Lenin but by Leon Trotsky. In October 1917, the 38-year-old Trotsky had been a Marxist revolutionary for 20 years but a member of the Bolshevik party for only a few months. He had been a member of the RSDLP before the split of 1903, but since then had not committed himself to either the Bolsheviks or the Mensheviks. In the years between 1903 and 1917 he had played a lone political hand, but if anything had leant towards the Mensheviks. During this period Lenin was harshly critical of Trotsky, but welcomed Trotsky's decision in July 1917 to join the Bolsheviks. He recognised that Trotsky's abilities and reputation made him an asset to the Bolshevik cause. Trotsky was an outstanding orator and – having been chairman of the St Petersburg soviet during the 1905 revolution – was a high-profile figure in revolutionary circles. In September 1917, Trotsky became Bolshevik chairman of the Petrograd soviet.

Acting through the MRC, Trotsky made it appear that power was being taken not by the Bolsheviks as such but rather by the Petrograd soviet. On 21 October the MRC secured control of Petrograd's ammunition dumps. On 24–25 October, forces loyal to the Bolsheviks occupied key points in the city. The Winter Palace, the Provisional Government's headquarters, was taken on 26 October. On the same day Lenin proclaimed the existence of a new government, the Council of People's Commissars – Sovnarkom (see p32, Figure 5), with himself at its head. Trotsky was named Commissar for Foreign Affairs, and Stalin Commissar for Nationalities. By this time Kerensky was no longer in

Petrograd. Realising what was afoot, he had fled the capital on 25 October and headed for the front in search of support from the army.

Popular uprising or coup d'etat?

The Bolsheviks claimed both in 1917 and afterwards that the October Revolution enjoyed mass support. In the History of the Communist Party of the Soviet Union (Short Course) prepared under Stalin's direction in 1939, for example, it was maintained that in October 1917 the workers and peasants came together in 'one common powerful revolutionary torrent'. This view of the October Revolution as a popular uprising was challenged at the time by the Mensheviks and SRs. Kerensky, for instance, claimed in early 1918 that the Bolsheviks were guilty of 'pure usurpation'. It has been challenged too by many non-communist historians. A recent example is the prominent right-wing American scholar Richard Pipes, who has argued that 'October was a classic coup d'etat, the capture of governmental power by a small minority … the vast majority of Russia's inhabitants at the time had no inkling of what had happened' (*The Russian Revolution*, 1990).

The best available evidence of the extent of the Bolsheviks' popularity in late 1917 is the result of the Constituent Assembly election (see below, Figure 2), which went ahead as scheduled in November. The Bolsheviks were, of course, opposed to the Constituent Assembly, but during their first weeks in power their position appeared so precarious they dared not risk provoking their enemies by calling the election off. All citizens over 20 years old were entitled to vote, and turnout was high. There appears to have been relatively little intimidation or electoral malpractice.

Figure 2
The result of the Constituent Assembly election, November 1917

	Votes cast	*Number of seats won*	*% share of the vote (rounded)*
SRs	21.8 million	438	53 %
Bolsheviks	10.0 million	168	24 %
Cadets	2.1 million	17	5 %
Mensheviks	1.4 million	18	3 %
Others/unaccounted	6.3 million	62	15 %
Totals	41.6 million	703	(100)

These results imply that support for the Bolsheviks in 1917 extended beyond Pipes' 'small minority' of the population. There are also grounds for arguing that their position was in some ways stronger than the overall result suggests. First, the Bolsheviks polled strongly in the major cities, especially in Petrograd. In some of the working-class districts of Petrograd, support for the Bolsheviks exceeded 70% of those voting. Second, ballot papers used in the election did not differentiate between the various elements of the SR party, which in the autumn of 1917 was disintegrating. The Left SRs temporarily became allies of the Bolsheviks. In late 1917, six Left SRs took up posts in Sovnarkom. A fair proportion of SR votes in the Constituent Assembly election, maybe as many as half, were cast for candidates who favoured collaboration with the Bolsheviks.

The extent of the Bolsheviks' popularity should not, however, be exaggerated. They were clearly a long way short of having majority support in Russia in late 1917. It should also be borne in mind that some of those who did support the Bolsheviks at this time were only lightly attached to the party. Public opinion in Russia in 1917 was fickle and volatile. Many of those who voted Bolshevik in the Constituent Assembly elections were fair-weather supporters who subsequently became disillusioned. One cause of disillusionment with the Bolsheviks after the October Revolution was their treatment of the Constituent Assembly when it met in January 1918. The Assembly was forcibly disbanded after it had been in session for a single day.

How important was Lenin's contribution to the success of the October Revolution?

◆ Without Lenin there would have been no October Revolution. Left to themselves, other Bolsheviks in the spring of 1917 would almost certainly not have thought in terms of making a bid for power. Instead they would probably have adopted the Menshevik position of support for the Provisional Government.

◆ The policies Lenin set out in the April Theses were the basis on which the Bolsheviks were able to increase their strength in the spring and early summer of 1917. The April Theses demonstrated Lenin's awareness of the mood of public opinion – an awareness that was remarkable given the fact that he had spent half a lifetime in exile and, in his own words, knew Russia only poorly.

◆ Lenin's demand for an uprising in the autumn of 1917 was decisive. Whether the other Bolsheviks would have gone ahead without his urgings is open to question.

◆ It would, however, be wrong to see Lenin's conduct in 1917 as a flawless exhibition of political manoeuvring. He miscalculated badly during the July Days – an episode Richard Pipes describes as his 'worst blunder'.

Studying the October Revolution

1 Write a paragraph explaining why each of the following were an asset to the Bolsheviks in 1917: (i) Lenin (ii) Trotsky (iii) the Kronstadt sailors (iv) the Red Guards (v) the Petrograd garrison.

2 Write a paragraph explaining the impact that the following had on the Bolsheviks' political prospects at the time: (i) the April Theses (ii) the July Days (iii) the Kornilov affair.

3 Make notes summarising (i) the strengths, and (ii) the weaknesses in 1917 of the Cadets, the SRs and the Mensheviks.

4 Write a paragraph on each of the following, explaining why they achieved prominence and what political errors they made: (i) P.N. Milyukov (ii) Alexander Kerensky (iii) Lavr Kornilov.

5 Make notes summarising (i) the arguments for, and (ii) the arguments against Richard Pipes' view that the October Revolution was 'a classic coup d'etat, the capture of governmental power by a small minority'.

3 Civil War and Allied intervention

How did the Bolshevik regime survive?

Key points

- The Civil War was highly complex, involving Greens, separatists and Allied forces as well as Reds and Whites
- After the Bolsheviks beat the Whites on three main fronts, they were attacked by Poles
- The Bolsheviks experimented in economic and military affairs, but when the Civil War began, this gave way to coercion and brutality
- 'Objective factors' and the Whites' failure to mobilise support were probably more important for the outcome of the Civil War than Lenin and Trotsky

The Russian Civil War was one of the most bitterly contested of all 20th-century wars. It cost over 3 million people their lives. A million or more died in the fighting, and more than 2 million as a result of disease. In addition, 2 million Russians left the country as political exiles. Something of what the war meant at a personal level can be seen in works by two Nobel Prize-winning Soviet novelists – *And Quiet Flows the Don* by Mikhail Sholokov (1905–1984) and *Doctor Zhivago* by Boris Pasternak (1890–1960).

The Russian Civil War was an episode of bewildering complexity. The central conflict was that between the Bolsheviks (or Reds) and the Whites, the term which the Bolsheviks used to refer to their conservative opponents because it was a colour historically associated with absolute monarchy. The Red–White conflict, however, was only part of the story. During the period of the Civil War the Bolsheviks also fought against 'Green' armies and against Russia's national minorities:

- The Greens were peasant forces. Some of them were associated with the SRs, and others were freelance units concerned mainly with the defence of their own locality. An example of the former is the SR 'People's Army', which fought against the Bolsheviks in Siberia in 1918. The best example of the latter is the 15,000 strong 'Revolutionary Insurgent Army of the Ukraine' led by the anarchist Nestor Makhno (1889–1935). Makhno's forces fought for the Bolsheviks against the Whites in 1919–20, but the Bolsheviks turned on him when he was of no further use to them.

- In his 'Declaration of the Rights of the Peoples of Russia' (November 1917) Lenin expressed a willingness to allow the Tsarist empire's non-Russian minorities to have rights of self-determination, including the right to separate themselves from Russia if they so wished. In practice, he was not prepared to see the population and resources of the minority areas lost to the Bolshevik state. Where breakaway regimes were set up, the Bolsheviks tried to overthrow them. Bolshevik armies, for example, fought against the Ukrainian separatist regime of Simon Petluria in 1918–20, Baltic (Estonian, Latvian and Lithuanian) separatists in 1918–19, and Transcaucasian (Armenian, Georgian, and Azerbaijani) separatists in 1920–21.

The War Begins, 1917–18

Early clashes

The first shots in the Russian Civil War were fired in October 1917, when army units loyal to Kerensky and commanded by General Krasnov advanced on Petrograd and were repulsed by the Bolsheviks. Bolshevik forces also saw action in late 1917 in the Volga region, where an anti-Bolshevik Volunteer Army had been assembled by Generals Alexeev and Kornilov. In comparison with what followed, however, these early clashes were small-scale affairs. The Civil War began in earnest as a result of two developments:

◆ The forcible dissolution of the Constituent Assembly by the Bolsheviks in January 1918. This outraged liberals and SRs who even after the October Revolution nursed hopes of a democratic political settlement.

◆ The treaty of Brest–Litovsk.

The treaty of Brest–Litovsk

Ending the war against Germany was Lenin's most pressing problem in late 1917. There were three main reasons why this was so:

◆ The Bolsheviks had promised peace before the October Revolution and could not go back on their promise without alienating their supporters.

◆ The Russian army, its strength draining away through desertions, was losing the ability to offer serious resistance to the Germans.

◆ The Bolsheviks wanted to be able to concentrate on overcoming their internal enemies. 'The bourgeoisie has to be throttled', said Lenin, 'and for that we need both hands free.'

Negotiations with Germany opened at Brest–Litovsk in November 1917. It soon became clear that a massive price would have to be paid for peace. Germany demanded the surrender of the Russian Poland, the Baltic provinces (Estonia, Latvia and Lithuania), Finland, the Ukraine and the southern Transcaucasus. These areas contained 26% of Russia's population, 27% of its arable land and 74% of its coal and iron ore.

The German terms threw the Bolshevik leadership into disarray. Left-wing Bolsheviks, headed by Bukharin (see p46, Key Reference), called for the rejection of the terms and the launching of a 'revolutionary war' against Germany. Trotsky, absurdly, argued for a policy of 'neither war nor peace', saying that Russia should declare the war to be at an end but refuse to sign a peace treaty with Germany. Lenin pressed for acceptance, claiming that Brest–Litovsk would only be a temporary setback, and got his way. The Brest–Litovsk treaty was signed on 3 March 1918.

Brest–Litovsk solved one of the Bolsheviks' problems, but exacerbated others. The Left SRs, deeply hostile to Brest–Litovsk, withdrew from Sovnarkom in protest. In June 1918, SRs· established the Committee of Members of the Constituent Assembly (known as 'Komuch') in the Urals region with the aim of overthrowing undemocratic Bolshevik rule and the Brest–Litovsk treaty.

The middle and upper classes, strongly nationalist in outlook, were also enraged by Brest–Litovsk. Efforts by the officer class of the army to put anti-Bolshevik forces into the field intensified. These efforts received support from Russia's wartime allies. The strategic interests of Britain and France demanded that an anti-German front in the East should be kept open if at all possible.

Whites versus Reds, 1918–20

The Czech Legion and Kolchak

In 1918 and early 1919, the principal military threat to the Bolsheviks was posed by the Czech Legion and the forces of Admiral Kolchak, based in the Urals region and Siberia.

The Czech Legion was 50,000 strong. Its members had originally been members of the Habsburg (Austro-Hungarian) army, but had either deserted to the Russians or had been taken prisoner by them. Believing that the defeat of Austro-Hungary would open the way to an independent Czechoslovakia, they fought alongside the Russians until Brest–Litovsk ended the war in the east. Arrangements were then made to transfer the Legion to western Europe via Siberia. In spring 1918, at Cheliabinsk on the Trans-Siberian railway, the Czechs overpowered their Bolshevik escorts. Britain and France, realising the Czechs' potential as a weapon against the Bolsheviks, encouraged them to fight, hoping that their efforts would contribute to the re-activation of the Eastern Front. The Czech Legion swiftly won control of most of western Siberia. By late 1918, however, weakened by mutinies and a lack of supplies, it ceased to be an effective fighting force.

Apart from the Czechs, there were two main anti-Bolshevik forces in the Urals region and Siberia in 1918. One was Komuch, and the other a White-dominated Siberian Regional Government based at Omsk. In-fighting between the two saw the defeat of Komuch and the expulsion of its SR members from Russia. The leadership of White forces in Siberia was assumed by Admiral Alexander Kolchak, formerly commander of Russia's Black Sea Fleet.

Kolchak was honest, but neurotic and lacking in political skill. However, in late 1918 and early 1919, Kolchak's 140,000-strong forces made spectacular progress, capturing Perm, Samara and Kazan, and threatening Moscow (see p20, Figure 3). A Bolshevik counter-offensive in May–July 1919 then forced them to retreat. After further defeats in late 1919, Kolchak fell into Bolshevik hands and was executed in February 1920.

Denikin and Wrangel

Following the deaths of Generals Kornilov (killed in action, April 1918) and Alexeev (heart attack, September 1918), command of the White 'Volunteer Army' in southern Russia passed to General Anton Denikin.

Denikin was brave, but lacked flair and political imagination. In late 1918,

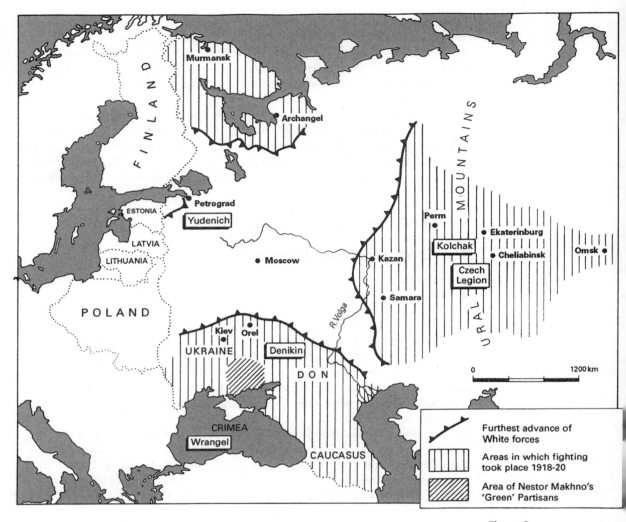

Figure 3
The Russian Civil War

Denikin had 150,000 men at his disposal. There were, however, tensions within his forces. The Armed Forces of Southern Russia (AFSR), the name by which Denikin's armies were known after November 1918, contained 40,000 Don Cossacks (descendants of runaway serfs who settled in the Don region from the 15th century onwards and developed a distinct identity), commanded by P.N. Krasnov, who were principally concerned with the defence of their homeland and cared little for the fate of Russia as a whole.

Despite these tensions, the AFSR were highly successful to begin with. In the summer and autumn of 1919 they advanced on a broad front, reaching Orel, only 250 miles from Moscow, in October (see above, Figure 3). They were then rolled backwards by a massive Bolshevik counter-attack. In March 1920, after retreat had degenerated into panic and collapse, Denikin resigned command of the AFSR and went into exile. He was replaced by Baron P.N.Wrangel.

In 1920, the remnants of the AFSR were bottled up on the Crimean peninsula. Though heavily outnumbered by the Bolshevik forces, they held out under Wrangel's leadership for nine months before admitting defeat. In November 1920, 150,000 civilian and military refugees, Wrangel among them, were evacuated from the Crimea in a fleet of Allied warships.

Yudenich

General Nikolai Yudenich's 15,000-strong North-Western Army was the smallest of the White forces. In 1919 it advanced out of its bases in Estonia, and in October (at about the same time Denikin reached Orel) came within sight of Petrograd. It was then defeated by a much larger Bolshevik force commanded by Trotsky. By the time it was threatened by Yudenich, Petrograd did not quite have the strategic importance it had once had, as Lenin had made Moscow the Bolshevik capital in March 1918. (The Bolsheviks were re-named the Communist Party in the same month.)

Allied intervention

Allied troops were originally sent to Russia to support efforts to re-open an Eastern Front against Germany. In November 1918 the war with Germany ended. Allied forces were not, however, withdrawn from Russia.

Allied politicians had different reasons for wanting a continuing military presence in Russia. A minority, headed by Winston Churchill, the British War Secretary, wanted to fight an ideological crusade against Bolshevism. Others saw a role for Allied troops in connection with a variety of limited objectives, such as protecting Allied munitions dumps at Archangel and Murmansk, rescuing the Czech Legion and supporting minorities struggling for independence from Russia. Opposed to continuing intervention were some powerful voices, notably Wilson, the US President, and the British Prime Minister Lloyd George.

Allied intervention after November 1918 was a half-hearted affair, reflecting the uncertainty and differences of opinion about its purposes. The troops of the most reluctant interventionist power, the United States, were more or less under orders to avoid involvement in combat. French forces were withdrawn from southern Russia in early 1919, only a few months after they had landed. The Japanese, primarily concerned with furthering their economic interests, confined themselves to Russia's Pacific coast and shunned contact with the Bolsheviks.

Britain was the most active of the interventionist powers. Four hundred British soldiers were killed in action in Russia in 1918–20. Three Victoria Crosses were awarded. In addition, Britain made supplies worth £100 million available to the Whites. Through incompetence and corruption though, a good deal of this material fell into Bolshevik hands. General Knox, the British military representative in Siberia, received a letter purporting to come from Trotsky, thanking him for his assistance in equipping the Red Army.

Figure 4
Allied forces in Russia, 1918–22

Region	Nationality	Numbers	Date of arrival	Date of departure
White Sea (Murmansk-Archangel)	British	10,000	March 1918	October 1919
	United States	5,000	Aug 1918	July 1919
	French, Canadians, Italians, Serbs	small detachments	mid-1918	Sept 1919
Baltic	British	naval squadron	Dec 1918	March 1920
Siberia	Czech Legion	55,000	May 1918	April 1920
	United States	12,000	Aug 1918	Jan 1920
	British	1,000	Aug 1918	Nov 1919
	Japanese	65,000	April 1918	October 1922
South (Crimea, Ukraine, Transcaucasus)	French	10,000	Dec 1918	April 1919
	Greeks	30,000	Dec 1918	April 1919
	Rumanians	30,000	Dec 1918	April 1919
	Poles	3,000	Dec 1918	April 1919
	British	1,000	Aug 1918	Dec 1919

The Russo-Polish war, 1920

The withdrawal of the Allies and the defeat of the Whites did not bring Lenin's troubles to an end. In 1920, Russia was attacked by Poland.

Poland in 1920 was a newly re-created state. In the late 18th century, it had lost its independence and had been partitioned among its three powerful neighbours – Russia, the Habsburg Empire and Prussia. The largest share went to Russia. In 1830 and 1863 Polish rebellions against Russian rule were brutally suppressed. At the end of the First World War, there was very little love lost between Poles and Russians.

The immediate Polish grievance in 1920 related to the border between Poland and Russia, proposed at the 1919 Paris peace conference by the Allies, who were instrumental in recreating Poland. The 'Curzon line', as it was known, failed to satisfy the ambitions of Pilsudski, the Polish leader, and he therefore resorted to armed force, attacking Soviet Russia in April 1920.

At first the war went badly from the Polish point of view, as the Red Army advanced to the outskirts of Warsaw. The Poles then won a crushing victory outside Warsaw, the so-called 'miracle of the Vistula', forcing the Red Army into headlong retreat. In October 1920, Russia agreed to a cease-fire, and under the subsequent treaty of Riga (1921) ceded more than 30,000 square miles of territory on its western border to Poland.

Bolshevik rule during the Civil War

The Red Army

At the time of the October Revolution, the Bolsheviks had about 50,000 men at their disposal – Red Guards, Latvian riflemen and Kronstadt sailors – but nothing resembling an organised army. When their enemies started to move against them, the Bolsheviks first thought in terms of creating an all-volunteer 'Socialist Guard' with elected commanders. Such a force, it was hoped, would sweep all before it by dint of revolutionary enthusiasm.

Lenin soon became impatient with this kind of idealistic thinking. In March 1918 Trotsky was appointed Commissar for War and became the principal architect of the Red Army. With Lenin's backing, he built the Red Army on traditional lines:

◆ Trotsky made extensive use of ex-Tsarist officers. In the Red Army they were referred to as *voenspets*, or 'military specialists'. Some ex-Tsarist officers joined the Red Army willingly. Others volunteered because they had no other way of making a living. Many were conscripted and were prevented from deserting by the threat of reprisals against their families. Every ex-Tsarist commander operated under the supervision of a political commissar, or minder, who was a Bolshevik of proven loyalty.

◆ Compulsory military service for the mass of the population was re-introduced in May 1918.

◆ Discipline in the Red Army was ferocious. Deserters and those guilty of unjustified retreat were liable to be executed.

By the end of 1918, there were 1 million men in the Red Army. In 1919, there were 3 million. By the time of the Russo-Polish war, there were 5.4 million. But in reality, the Red Army was not as formidable as these numbers might suggest. Many of its units were poorly trained and equipped. Desertion was a continuous problem. In mid-1919, for example, men were deserting at the rate of 250,000 a month. The Red Army was also ravaged by disease: in 1920 30% of its men contracted typhus.

War Communism

The Bolsheviks' earliest initiatives in economic policy were designed to ensure their regime's short-term survival. Quite simply, the workers and peasants were given what they wanted. The Land Decree (November 1917) legitimised the peasant land seizures of 1917, and the Decree on Workers' Control (November 1917) effectively handed the management of factories over to shop stewards and trades unionists.

These policies soon proved to be unsustainable. The treaty of Brest–Litovsk and the spread of civil war deprived the Bolsheviks of industrial plant, raw materials and arable land. In what was sometimes called Sovdepia (Bolshevik-held territory), industrial output slumped and there were shortages of food and fuel in the cities. Prices soared. During the Civil War, Sovdepia experienced catastrophic levels of inflation. The value of the rouble collapsed more or less completely. As a result, the peasantry were unwilling to sell their produce for paper money. This made the shortage of food in the towns even worse. Desperate for food, urban workers deserted the cities in massive numbers and returned to their native villages. In 1918–20, Petrograd lost three-quarters of its population. The population of Moscow halved during the same period. On top of their other difficulties, factories were faced with a dearth of labour.

In these circumstances, the Bolsheviks resorted to a series of coercive measures, together known as War Communism:

◆ In the course of 1918, industry was brought under state control. After 1918, nationalised industries operated under the overall supervision of the Supreme Council of National Economy, or Vesenkha (see p32, Figure 5), which had been established in December 1917. Headed by A.I. Rykov, later a prominent victim of Stalin's 'show trials', the Vesenkha was attached to Sovnarkom. Individual industries were controlled by departments, or *glavki*, of the Vesenkha.

◆ Discipline was re-asserted in the factories. The nationalisation of industry saw a return to 'one-man management' in place of control by workers' councils. In addition, the Bolsheviks introduced internal passports in an attempt to halt the flight of industrial workers to the countryside. Trotsky wanted to tighten control over industrial workers even further by creating a labour army which would work under military discipline. Lenin, however, overruled him.

◆ From 1918 onwards, food was requisitioned from the peasantry by the state. 'Food brigades' were sent out from the towns to extract grain from the peasantry, and where necessary, the Red Army and the Cheka (see p32, Figure 5) were used. In practice, 'requisitioning' often meant the straightforward theft of grain.

◆ Rationing was introduced. The way in which rationing worked reflected the Bolsheviks' priorities and values. The biggest rations went to Red Army soldiers and workers in heavy industry. Then came civil servants and workers in light industry, who received scarcely enough to live on. At the bottom of the scale were 'capitalists, landlords and parasites' – in practice, the middle classes – who, said Zinoviev, were given 'just enough bread so as not to forget the smell of it'.

The Red Terror

The Bolsheviks began to take action against their political opponents as early as November 1917, when dozens of Cadet leaders were arrested and imprisoned as 'enemies of the people'. A few weeks later (December 1917) a political police force was established, the 'All-Russian Extraordinary Commission for Struggle against Counter-Revolution and Sabotage', or Cheka.

The Cheka was headed by 'Iron' Felix Dzerzhinsky (see p46, Key Reference), a Bolshevik of Polish landed gentry origin. In 1917 Lenin may have thought of the Cheka as a temporary expedient, but under a variety of names (it was renamed the GPU, or State Political Administration, in 1922) it became a permanent feature of Communist rule in Russia. The Cheka operated outside the law. Its victims were not given the benefit of a trial and had no right of appeal against its actions.

From the outset, the Cheka had a reputation for savagery. The most notorious of its early actions was the murder of Tsar Nicholas II and his family en masse at Ekaterinburg in the Urals (July 1918). The worst atrocities came after an attempt on Lenin's life in August 1918, when an SR, Fanya Kaplan, shot him in the neck from close range. The methods used by the Cheka in the mass terror which followed the assassination attempt included executions, imprisonment in labour camps, hostage-taking and torture of the most gruesome kind. 'We are exterminating the bourgeoisie as a class', declared Dzerzhinsky's lieutenant, Martyn Latsis, in November 1918.

The Red Terror was condemned by the Whites and the Allies, but it should be noted that there was a 'White Terror' too. Kolchak terrorised peasants to fight in his armies, while in the Ukraine in 1918–19 Denikin's forces took part in anti-Semitic pogroms which cost tens of thousands of Jews their lives.

Why did the Bolsheviks win the Civil War?

'Objective factors'

Historians of the Civil War have used the term 'objective factors' to refer to the resources available to the combatants and to their geographical position. There were three main 'objective factors' which advantaged the Bolsheviks:

◆ The Bolsheviks controlled the most heavily-populated parts of Russia. In 1918–19, Bolshevik-held territory contained some 70 million people, compared with approximately 20 million in the White-controlled areas. The Bolsheviks therefore had a bigger reservoir of manpower upon which to draw than the Whites. One consequence of this was that in major battles, the Red Army invariably had a huge numerical advantage over its opponents.

◆ As a result of its participation in the First World War, Russia was awash with munitions and other war material at the time of the October Revolution. In 1917–18 almost all of the arsenal of the old Tsarist army – one estimate suggests something like 2.5 million rifles, 12,000 artillery pieces and 28 million shells – fell into Bolshevik hands. The Bolsheviks did not, of course, rely solely on this windfall. Russia's main engineering and armaments factories were located within Sovdepia and this gave them the capacity to manufacture new weapons.

◆ The Bolsheviks controlled the hub of the Russian railway network, which radiated outwards from Moscow. This enabled the Bolsheviks to rush reinforcements to battle fronts where they were threatened. The Whites, by contrast, had to operate around the circumference of Bolshevik-held territory. Communication between the different White armies was extremely limited, and as a result it was all but impossible for White commanders to co-ordinate their strategies.

Richard Pipes believes the 'objective factors' were so heavily in the Bolsheviks' favour that the outcome of the Civil War was a 'foregone conclusion' (*Russia under the Bolshevik Regime*, 1994). Other historians, for example Orlando Figes (A *People's Tragedy*, 1996), though acknowledging the importance of 'objective factors', have doubted whether they were quite as decisive as Pipes alleges.

The failure of the Whites to mobilise mass support

There were two main reasons for the failure of the White generals to mobilise an extensive following:

◆ Their attitude to the land issue. Influenced by the landowners among their supporters, Kolchak and Denikin made plain their belief in the rights of property. Peasants were left in little doubt that a White victory would mean the restoration to its former owners of the land they had seized in 1917. Bolshevik propaganda was swift to play upon peasant fears.

◆ Their particular brand of nationalism. They believed in 'A Russia Great, United and Indivisible'. They aimed, in other words, to re-establish the Russian empire with its pre-1917 borders. As a result, the Whites were unwilling to make concessions of any kind to separatism. This presented them with problems because some of the areas in which they were based – the Ukraine and the Transcaucasus, for example – were areas in which separatist feeling was strong. Ukrainians and Georgians intent on self-government could not be expected to throw their lot in with White commanders who were openly hostile to their aspirations. Denikin was not even prepared to offer autonomy to the Don Cossacks, despite the fact that Cossack soldiers were vital to his success.

It is not altogether surprising that Denikin and Kolchak were incapable of mobilising support. They were soldiers, not politicians. They had no insight into popular opinion and underestimated the importance of propaganda. There were politicians who attached themselves to the headquarters of the White commanders, but for the most part they were squabbling mediocrities.

Bolshevik strengths

The Bolsheviks were certainly not successful in the Civil War because they themselves enjoyed massive popularity. R. Bruce Lockhart, a British intelligence agent operating in Russia in the early part of the Civil War period, estimated in late 1918 that Bolshevik supporters numbered no more than 10% of the population. However, the Bolsheviks did appear to many Russians as defenders of the gains of 1917 against those who wished to turn the clock back. When the Civil War crystallised into a Red–White conflict, this proved to be an important advantage. Faced with a choice between Reds and Whites, peasants, fearful of losing land, sided with the Reds.

The Bolsheviks were also effectively led. Lenin's role in the Civil War period was in some respects a muted one – he remained in Moscow throughout, never visiting any of the battle fronts – but he influenced thinking on strategy, offered unwavering support to those implementing the 'Red Terror' and, above all, was a hard-headed decision-maker when the need arose. His capacity to make tough decisions was shown most clearly when he forced through acceptance of the Brest–Litovsk treaty in the face of stiff opposition from other leading Bolsheviks.

Lenin's contribution to victory in the Civil War was equalled, perhaps surpassed, by Trotsky's. Trotsky may not have been a great battlefield commander, but he was a brilliant organiser. He was also an inspirational figure, moving from front to front in his famous armoured train, rallying Red forces with rousing oratory.

Studying the Russian Civil War

1 The aims of the main Russian participants need to be understood. Write a paragraph each on (i) the Bolsheviks (ii) the Whites and (iii) the Greens, summarising the kind of political and economic arrangements each aimed to introduce in Russia.

2 During the Civil War era, the Bolsheviks faced enemies of differing importance at different times. Produce (in tabular form) a set of notes on Germany, the Czech Legion, Kolchak, Denikin, Yudenich and the Poles, showing (i) the date at which each of these enemies posed its most serious threat to the Bolsheviks, and (ii) the way in which the Bolsheviks removed or overcame each of these threats. In addition, rank these six enemies of the Bolsheviks in order of importance, giving reasons for your choice.

3 'War Communism and Trotsky's creation of the Red Army involved a departure from the ideas and policies with which the Bolsheviks had been associated when they first came into power.' What evidence can be offered in support of this claim?

4 What arguments can be offered which (i) support, and (ii) challenge Richard Pipes' view that the outcome of the Russian Civil War was a foregone conclusion because the Bolsheviks controlled most of Russia's resources?

5 In the last part of this chapter, three reasons are given for the Bolsheviks' success in the Civil War: (i) 'objective factors' (ii) the failure of the Whites to mobilise mass support (iii) Bolshevik strengths. Rank these three reasons in order of importance, explaining your choice.

4 The crisis of 1921

Why did Lenin introduce the New Economic Policy and what were its consequences?

Key points

◆ In 1921 the Bolsheviks were forced into an economic U-turn
◆ The NEP (New Economic Policy) created a mixed economy in Russia
◆ Economic freedom was accompanied by tighter political control
◆ The NEP served its political purpose and brought economic recovery

---

The defeat of Wrangel and the end of the Russo-Polish war in late 1920 brought no respite for the Bolshevik regime. In 1921, the Bolsheviks were confronted with an internal crisis of major proportions. The crisis was of their own making. Its immediate cause was intense and widespread hostility to the policy of War Communism, but it owed much to disillusionment of a general kind with Bolshevik rule as well. Lenin handled the crisis adroitly but his response to it – the introduction of the New Economic Policy – was viewed with misgivings by many of his fellow Bolsheviks.

Challenges to Bolshevism, 1921

During the Civil War, the hostility of the peasantry towards grain requisitioning was to some extent held in check by fears of a White victory. But in 1920, as the fighting wound down and a poor harvest reduced villages to near starvation, it boiled over. By 1921, much of countryside was in a state of open revolt against Bolshevik rule. The fiercest fighting took place in Tambov province, to the south of Moscow, where a 40,000-strong peasant force led by Alexander Antonov waged a guerrilla campaign against the Red Army. The Red Army's response was brutal in the extreme. Among other things, it used poisoned gas against the rebels and took thousands of wives and children hostage. The uprisings in Tambov and elsewhere brought Russia close to paralysis. Large parts of the country were effectively out of the authorities' control. Railway transport was seriously disrupted. There was a food crisis in the towns. The Red Army was stretched to the limit. In these circumstances, Lenin had little alternative but to think in terms of concessions to the peasantry.

Rural discontent had its parallel in the towns. Urban protest was largely fuelled by the shortage of food, but there was also resentment over the privileges of Communist Party members and calls for the restoration of trade union rights. Strikes and demonstrations in Moscow forced the authorities to impose martial law, while in Petrograd thousands of workers refused to work.

In both cities there were clashes between troops and demonstrators in which people were killed.

The Bolsheviks suffered a further blow in March 1921 when the 10,000 sailors of the Baltic fleet based at Kronstadt mutinied in support of the Petrograd strikers. The mutineers published a fifteen-point manifesto (sometimes called the Petropavlovsk Resolution, named after the battleship where it was agreed), in which Bolshevik rule was bitterly condemned. They demanded the legalisation of all socialist and anarchist parties, freshly-elected soviets, rights for trades unions and an end to Communist privileges. The Kronstadt mutiny only lasted for a fortnight – it was suppressed by 50,000 Red Army troops who staged a frontal assault on the island across the icebound Gulf of Finland, 10,000 of them killed in the process – but it was, from the Bolshevik point of view, a profoundly embarrassing episode. In 1917 the Kronstadters had been among the Bolsheviks' strongest supporters. Trotsky had called them 'the pride and glory of the Russian revolution'. Their mutiny in 1921 showed just how extensive disillusionment with the Bolsheviks had become.

The New Economic Policy

Economic changes

In March 1921, Lenin announced that *prodraszverstka* (grain requisitioning) was to be abandoned. This was the first step in the introduction of the New Economic Policy (NEP). Other changes followed in piecemeal fashion until the end of 1922. The overall effect of the introduction of NEP was to create a mixed economy in Soviet Russia, with both a public (state-controlled) sector and a private sector which operated on the basis of the market forces of supply and demand.

The NEP had four main features:

◆ Grain requisitioning was replaced by a 'tax in kind'. This meant that peasants had to hand over a fixed proportion of their grain to the state. Any surplus left over after this 'tax in kind' had been paid could then be sold for profit on the open market. The amount of grain demanded by the state in 1921 totalled about half the amount requisitioned in 1920. In 1924 the 'tax in kind' was replaced by payments in the form of money.

◆ Private trading and the private ownership of small-scale businesses were legalised. Many of the privately-owned businesses which emerged after the introduction of the NEP were in the service sector, but there was also a significant amount of private manufacturing typically producing consumer goods such as clothes and footwear.

◆ The 'commanding heights' of the economy, as Lenin called them, remained under state control. These included not only heavy industries like coal and steel, but also the railway network and the banking system. Foreign trade continued to be a state monopoly.

◆ The industries which remained under state control after 1921–22 were expected to trade at a profit, and if they got into difficulties they were not baled out by the government. One of the consequences of this new regime was an increase in unemployment, which was caused by industries shedding surplus workers in order to increase efficiency.

Political repression

Many in the Bolshevik ranks were dismayed by the New Economic Policy. They viewed it as an about-turn, away from socialism and towards capitalism. Lenin himself admitted as much. 'In 1917', he told the Eleventh Party Congress (see p32, Figure 5) in 1922, 'the key to the situation was to get out of the war. In 1919 and 1920 the key was military resistance. In 1921 the key was orderly retreat'. Bukharin, editor of *Pravda*, was even more blunt. He called the NEP 'a peasant Brest–Litovsk' – a surrender for the sake of survival.

The misgivings of the NEP's critics were reinforced after 1921 by the emergence of a class of get-rich-quick private traders known as 'nepmen', and by the re-opening of bars, nightclubs and casinos in Russia's major cities. 'We felt betrayed', recalled a one-time Bolshevik in 1945. Some disillusioned party members put it about that the initials NEP really stood for 'New Exploitation of the Proletariat'.

Lenin's response to criticism from within the Bolshevik ranks was to stifle it. In 1921, a ban was introduced on the formation of factions (groups with their own organisation and ideas on policy) within the party. This effectively ended the Bolshevik tradition of open debate until a decision was reached.

The ban on factions was followed by a major purge of the party's membership. On the eve of the introduction of the NEP there were 730,000 party members, but by early 1923 there were only 500,000 (see Key Reference, Table 2). The message to those who survived the purge was clear. The decisions of the leadership were to be accepted without question.

The imposition of tighter discipline within the Bolshevik party was part of a wider political clampdown which followed the introduction of the NEP. In 1921 5,000 'counter-revolutionary' Mensheviks were arrested. In 1922 thirty-four prominent SRs were put on trial in Moscow, accused of terrorist activities: eleven of them were condemned to death. Other highly publicised trials in 1922 saw prominent churchmen in the dock on conspiracy charges. Through these 'show trials' Lenin signalled that economic freedom was not going to be accompanied by any relaxation of the Bolsheviks' political grip on Russia.

The Soviet economy after 1921

Famine

In the summer of 1921, a drought in southern Russia led to major crop failures. The option of falling back on supplies of grain set aside for emergencies was not open to peasant households, because their reserves had been seized in the Bolsheviks' requisitioning programme. The result was a famine affecting 25 million people. The death toll may have reached as high as 5 million. 'The 1921 famine in Russia was the greatest human disaster in European history, other than those caused by war, since the Black Death' (Richard Pipes, *Russia under the Bolshevik Regime* 1919–1924, 1994). In desperation, some people resorted to cannibalism.

Recovery

From Lenin's point of view, the NEP was a success both politically and economically. Politically it took the steam out of peasant discontent. Economically it brought about recovery. By the time of Lenin's death, the output of industry was rising sharply and grain production had risen well above the catastrophically low levels of 1920–21, though pre-war production levels had not been reached in either industry or agriculture (see Key Reference, Table 1).

The 'scissors crisis'

The recovery of the Soviet economy after 1921 was in some respects erratic and uncertain. Difficulties arose in 1923 as a result of the different growth rates of agriculture and industry. Industrial goods were in shorter supply than foodstuffs, which meant they were more expensive. The result was the 'scissors crisis' – so named (by Trotsky) because the lines on a graph showing trends in agricultural and industrial prices resembled a pair of scissors being opened. The government acted to correct the imbalance, pushing industrial prices down.

The debate on economic strategy

The 'scissors crisis' was a short-term problem. A bigger problem facing the Bolsheviks was the question of how long the capitalistic NEP should last.

On this, opinion was divided. Bukharin, one of the party's leading economic theorists, wanted the NEP to be made permanent. Opposed to him was E.A. Preobrazhensky, another prominent economic guru, who wanted to abandon the NEP in favour of a programme of industrialisation which was to be financed by squeezing the peasantry. This line was backed by Trotsky, whereas Stalin appeared to side with Bukharin.

Lenin positioned himself between these opposed viewpoints. He declared in December 1921: 'We will carry out this policy [the NEP] seriously and for a long time, but, of course, not forever'. The issue of long-term economic strategy was unresolved at the time of his death.

Studying the crisis of 1921

1 Explain the meaning of the following terms, writing one or two sentences on each: (i) mixed economy (ii) 'tax in kind' (iii) the 'commanding heights' of the economy (iv) 'nepmen' (v) factions.

2 What specific features of the Bolsheviks' rule, other than grain requisitioning, contributed to the widespread disillusionment which existed in 1921?

3 Look back at pp27–28 and the section entitled Challenges to Bolshevism, 1921. Three main elements in the crisis facing Lenin in 1921 are listed as bullet points. Which of these do you think had (i) the most, and (ii) the least influence on his decision to change Soviet Russia's economic course? Give reasons for your choice.

4 'In 1921 the Bolsheviks abandoned extremism and repression and embarked on a new, moderate course'. Summarise the arguments which can be offered (i) for, and (ii) against this view. Is it a view you would accept or reject? Give reasons for your choice.

5 Government and society in Lenin's Russia

How free was Russia under Lenin?

Key points

- ◆ Under Lenin, people were deprived of the right to take part in the political process
- ◆ Political power under Lenin became increasingly centralised
- ◆ Organised religion was attacked by the Bolsheviks
- ◆ Bolshevism was liberal in matters of sex and morality

In April 1917, following the introduction by the Provisional Government of a series of measures designed to guarantee basic liberties, Lenin declared that Russia was one of the freest countries in the world. In truth, under the Bolshevik regime Russians were stripped of most of the rights they briefly enjoyed in 1917. The repressive character of Bolshevik rule was most apparent in the political sphere. By 1924 the mass of the people had effectively been deprived of all worthwhile political rights.

The Bolsheviks did not, however, eliminate freedom and individual choice in all areas of Russian life. Organised religion came under serious attack, but in other areas, notably that of sexual morality, Bolshevik rule was more liberal. Soviet citizens were also given significant economic freedoms under the NEP, but many of them no doubt feared – correctly, as it turned out – that these would be short-lived rather than permanent.

Government

One-party state

Lenin's Russia was in spirit a one-party state, more or less from the outset. The Cadets were outlawed in November 1917, their newspapers having been shut down within days of the October seizure of power. The SRs and Mensheviks were barred from openly taking part in political activity in June 1918, though they were able to lead a shadowy, semi-legal existence during the Civil War years. They were finally driven underground, and their leaders either arrested or forced into exile, in 1921–22.

The centralisation of power

In 1917, the Bolsheviks (who renamed themselves the Communist Party in

STATE INSTITUTIONS

Council of People's Commissars (Sovnarkom)
Formed on 26 October 1917. Originally 15 members with Lenin as its chairman, membership grew to 20 or so. Members of Sovnarkom were in theory chosen by the Central Executive Committee. According to the 1918 constitution, Sovnarkom had responsibility for the 'general direction' of public affairs in the RSFSR. It also had the power to issue orders and decrees, so there was no clear line of division between its responsibilities and those of the Central Executive Committee, which also had responsibilities in the law-making sphere.

All-Russian Central Executive Committee
Elected by Congress of Soviets to exercise authority on its behalf when it was not in session. In theory co-ordinated all the legislative and administrative work of the government.

Cheka
'All-Russian Extraordinary Commission for Struggle against Counter-Revolution and Sabotage'. Soviet Russia's political police, founded in December 1917 and headed by Dzerzhinsky. Nominally attached to Sovnarkom, but in practice Dzerzhinsky was answerable to Lenin personally and (after 1919) to the Politburo. Renamed the GPU (State Political Administration) in 1922.

Vesenkha
Supreme Council of the National Economy. Formed in December 1917 and attached to Sovnarkom. Function was to organise the national economy and state finances. Less important after the introduction of the NEP than previously.

All-Russian Congress of Soviets
In theory had supreme law-making authority. Met twice (later reduced to once) each year. Composed of delegates elected by city and provincial soviets. Representation weighted heavily in favour of the cities, the home of the workers.

City and Provincial Soviets
The right to take part in elections to soviets was confined to those who earned their living by 'production or socially useful labour'. The soviets were 'local organs of power' with, in theory, independence in local matters.

COMMUNIST PARTY INSTITUTIONS

Politburo
Founded in 1919. The inner ruling group of the Communist Party. Became the key decision-making body in Soviet affairs. Between 1919 and 1922 had 5 members and 3 'candidate' or probationary members. After 1922 had 7 members and 2 or 3 candidate members. Members chosen by the Central Committee.

Orgburo
The Organisational Bureau. Founded in 1919 and, like the Politburo, a sub-committee of the Central Committee. Supposed to deal with organisational matters while the Politburo decided policy. Lost ground to the Party Secretariat in the early 1920s.

Secretariat
Initially subordinate to Orgburo, but grew extremely powerful after Stalin became its head in 1922. Controlled appointments to Communist Party posts in the provinces.

Central Committee
Members were elected by the Party Congress. Membership in 1917 was 29 (21 full members and 8 'candidate' or non-voting members) but by 1922 had risen to 45 (27 full and 18 candidate members). In and before 1917 the Central Committee was the key decision-making body in Party affairs, but after 1919 was supplanted by the Politburo. Full meetings of the Central Committee became increasingly infrequent.

Party Congress
In the years between its formation in 1898 and the seizure of power, only 6 full Party Congresses, or conferences, were held. During the period of Lenin's rule in Russia Congresses were held annually, but after Stalin established himself in power this pattern was broken: the 17th Congress was held in 1932, the 18th in 1939 and the 19th in 1952. The Party Congress elected the Central Committee to supervise the Party's affairs between Congresses.

Local Communist Parties

March 1918) had to construct a system of government largely from scratch. In their early days in power they improvised. They created organisations which met their immediate needs, and did not worry too much about administrative tidiness. There was in consequence some overlap between the jurisdiction of different bodies, and lines of accountability were sometimes blurred.

However, between 1917 and 1922, government in Bolshevik Russia took on a progressively clearer shape (see p32, Figure 5). During these years, two distinct trends were evident:

◆ The Communist Party's growth in importance, at the expense of the institutions of the Soviet state. By 1924 the role of state bodies amounted to little more than the implementation of decisions which had been made within the Party hierarchy.

◆ The erosion of internal democracy within the Communist Party and the concentration of power in an increasingly small number of hands.

During the first year or so of Bolshevik rule, the key decision-making body in the Soviet state was Sovnarkom, which was in theory responsible to the people at large via the All-Russian Congress of Soviets (see p32, Figure 5). In 1917–18 it met daily under Lenin's strict and efficient chairmanship. In 1919–20 though, following the Bolsheviks' decision at their Eighth Congress (1919) to strengthen the party's machinery, Sovnarkom began to lose ground to Party institutions, notably to the newly-established Politburo (see p32, Figure 5).

An example of Sovnarkom's decline was the Communist Party's declaration in 1919 that the Cheka was its 'direct organ' and was accountable to no one else. By 1921 Sovnarkom was meeting only once a week, and People's Commissars got into the habit of sending their deputies to its meetings rather than attending in person. Sovnarkom's decline was matched by the marginalisation of the soviets. At grass roots level, the local Communist Party secretary had become a far more important figure than the chairman of the local soviet by the early 1920s. In addition, elections to soviets were little more than charades in the 1920s because non-members of the Communist Party were barred from offering themselves as candidates.

The emergence of the Politburo after 1919 as a kind of 'inner cabinet' marked not only a decline in the importance of state institutions, but also a growing centralisation of power within the Communist Party. Before the establishment of the Politburo, the most influential body in Communist Party affairs was the large and unwieldy Central Committee, which had thirty to forty members in comparison with the Politburo's eight or nine. Under rules laid down in 1919 the Politburo was to be accountable to the Central Committee, but it soon became clear that these rules meant little.

The rise of the Politburo was not the only way in which the power of the Communist Party's leaders in the early 1920s grew at the expense of its rank-and-file members. After 1919, it became increasingly common for the national leadership – working through the Party's Secretariat (see p32, Figure 5), headed after 1922 by Stalin – to fill posts in the localities with its own nominees, depriving local Party committees of power over appointments. Also extremely important in this context was the 1921 ban on factions, which limited the ability of rank-and-file Party members to challenge the leadership's decisions.

At the end of his life Lenin became deeply uneasy about the amount of power wielded by senior Communist Party officials. In 1923, he published a scheme to dilute the power of the bureaucrats by making them more

Figure 5
The organs of government and of the Communist Party under Lenin

accountable to ordinary Communist Party members. By this stage though, he was too ill to enforce his wishes.

National minorities

When the Bolsheviks were in opposition in 1917, they promised to respect the right of Russia's national minorities to independence and self-government. This promise was incorporated into the two Soviet constitutions of the Lenin era. The first of these constitutions, laid down in July 1918, created the Russian Socialist Federated Soviet Republic, or RSFSR. The RSFSR was the official name of the Bolshevik state for the first six years of its existence. The second constitution, drafted in the early 1920s following the end of hostilities in the Civil War, finally came into operation in 1924. It added three nominally independent republics – the Ukraine, Belorussia and the Transcaucasus – to the RSFSR to form the Union of Soviet Socialist Republics (USSR), the name by which the Soviet state was known until its disintegration in 1991. The 1924 constitution laid it down that each member-state had the right to leave the Union if it so wished, but in practice this undertaking was worthless. The reality was that Russia's national minorities were no better off under the Communists than they had been under the Tsars.

Society

Religion

The Bolsheviks were atheists. They viewed organised religion as an instrument used by the ruling class to deceive the masses into accepting their inferiority and poverty without complaint. In consequence, they believed that a successful onslaught on religious belief would liberate the people from damaging superstition. The Bolsheviks also believed that the Russian Orthodox Church, the church of two-thirds of the population, was a counter-revolutionary body. This latter belief resulted from the Orthodox Church's closeness to Tsarism. In Tsarist Russia, it had been the official state church and had received extensive subsidies from public funds to support its educational work.

In 1917–18 the Orthodox Church came under fierce attack, losing its privileged status and much of its wealth. In late 1917 its lands were nationalised and it lost control of its schools. In early 1918 the 'Decree on Freedom of Conscience and on Church and Religious Associations' separated the Church from the state, banned it from owning property (its buildings were in future to be rented from local soviets) and outlawed the teaching of religion to those under eighteen. Raids on churches by Red Army units or Red Guards, in which objects of value were seized and resistance brutally suppressed, became common. In late 1918 all monasteries were closed down and their assets seized while the Patriarch, or head, of the Orthodox Church, Tikhon, was temporarily placed under house arrest. When Tikhon had been elected to his position in 1917 he had hoped to keep the church out of politics, but given the Bolsheviks' attitude towards religion, there was never the remotest prospect that his hopes would be fulfilled.

In 1921–22, the Bolsheviks intensified their campaign against religion. The pretext for this new offensive was a claim that the Orthodox Church had refused to sell its valuables to assist famine victims. Soviets were therefore

Figure 6
Bolshevik anti-religious propaganda: 'The spider and his prey', a poster published in 1920. The spider is the Orthodox Church and his prey the people – who mistakenly trust the spider.

ordered to remove all precious items from churches in their localities. In many places, priests and congregations resisted these confiscations. This led to clashes with the authorities in which some 8,000 people were killed. There followed two major 'show trials' in Moscow and Petrograd, in which prominent churchmen were accused of organising counter-revolution. These show trials were accompanied by a programme of harassment and ridicule of worshippers carried out by Komsomol, the Young Communist movement.

Women, divorce and abortion

In sharp contrast to the Bolsheviks' intolerance of religion was their liberal-mindedness in matters relating to marriage and sexual conduct. Soon after coming to power, they swept away the restrictions on divorce and abortion that had existed in Tsarist Russia. The Bolsheviks' Family Code of 1918 laid it down that a marriage could be dissolved at the request of either partner without any need for grounds – such as desertion, cruelty or adultery – to be given. No other European country at the time had a divorce law anything like as liberal as that set out in the Family Code. Abortion, strictly prohibited in

Tsarist Russia, was legalised in 1920 and was made available free of charge in Soviet hospitals. This again was far less restrictive than anything that existed elsewhere in Europe.

The Bolshevik attitude to divorce and abortion had a number of origins. One was a belief in the cause of women's equality. Another was the view held in some Bolshevik quarters that the family was an outdated institution. There were also some prominent Bolsheviks who had little time for conventional or 'bourgeois' norms in sexual matters and who viewed sex in a matter-of-fact way as a natural impulse to be assuaged, like hunger or thirst. Particularly associated with the latter view was Alexandra Kollontai (1872–1952), daughter of a wealthy general and People's Commissar for Social Welfare in Lenin's government. Kollontai's own liaisons, in particular her marriage to a Bolshevik sailor twenty years her junior, were the subject of a good deal of malicious gossip in the upper reaches of the Communist Party.

Soviet citizens, the urban population in particular, were quick to take advantage of the new divorce and abortion laws. In the mid-1920s Soviet Russia had the highest divorce rate in Europe – three times higher than Germany and twenty-five times higher than the United Kingdom. Abortion too became common, especially in Russia's major cities. In the course of 1926, nearly five per cent of all women of child-bearing age in Moscow had an abortion. By the early 1930s Soviet doctors were performing 1.5 million abortions each year.

The extent to which Soviet women were liberated by the changes introduced by the Bolsheviks is open to question. Women deserted by the fathers of their children frequently had to struggle to get child support payments from them. The equality of men and women before the law enshrined in the 1918 Family Code did not prevent women losing out to men in competition for jobs, nor did it lead to equal pay for equal work. There is no evidence to suggest that the male partners of working women in Lenin's Russia did their share of housework. In the countryside, life went on much as before.

The arts and censorship

The Bolsheviks came to power at a time of exceptional creativity in the arts in Russia. At work in the visual arts were the likes of Kandinsky, Chagall, Malevich and Rodchenko. In literature there was the poet Alexander Blok and the novelist Maxim Gorky, in music the composers Prokofiev and Rachmaninoff, and in the theatre the directors Stanislavski and Sergei Eisenstein, the latter eventually becoming better known as a film-maker.

Initially the Bolsheviks, though swift to make use of the visual arts for propaganda purposes, allowed writers and artists a fair amount of latitude. Gorky, for example, was permitted in 1917–18 to sound off at the Bolsheviks in his magazine *Novaya Zhizn* (New Life). The Bolsheviks' comparatively relaxed attitude was due in large part to the fact that Anatoly Lunarcharsky, the People's Commissar for Public Enlightenment – in effect, Minister for education and the arts – was a cultured and comparatively open-minded figure who accepted that artists needed a measure of freedom from political control. Lunarcharsky's indulgence was not, however, enough to prevent many writers and artists from leaving the country during and after the Civil War period.

State control of the arts tightened in the early 1920s. During the Civil War era censorship in Russia was patchy and inefficient, but in 1922 it was put on to a new footing when the Directorate for Literature and Publishing, popularly known as Glavlit, was formed. After 1922, all items intended for publication needed a licence from Glavlit before they could appear. Glavlit also had responsibilities for suppressing 'underground' literature. Here it worked closely with the Cheka. Glavlit's censors, says Richard Pipes, had a 'devastating' effect on creativity because writers, aware of the censors' power, learned to practise self-censorship.

The pockets of freedom and experimentation which existed in Lenin's Russia ceased to exist in the Stalin era. Under Stalin, the work of writers and artists had to conform to the official doctrine of 'Socialist Realism'. In education, where there had been an emphasis on co-operative learning and project work under Lunarcharsky in the early 1920s, there was a return to traditional methods. In 1936, abortion was effectively outlawed and divorce made much more difficult to obtain.

Studying government and society in Lenin's Russia

1 Make notes summarising the role and importance in Soviet government by 1921 of the following institutions: (i) Sovnarkom (ii) the Politburo (iii) the Communist Party Secretariat (iv) local soviets.

2 What arguments can be offered in support of the view that after 1921, the top echelon of Communist Party leaders were not accountable to anyone at all?

3 Make notes explaining the reasons for (i) the Bolsheviks' hostility to the Russian Orthodox Church, and (ii) the Bolsheviks' relatively liberal attitude towards divorce and abortion.

4 'Both in theory and in practice the Bolsheviks were strongly committed to the cause of women's equality'. What evidence can be offered (i) for, and (ii) against this view?

5 'In Lenin's Russia all individual rights and freedoms were suppressed'. Would you agree or disagree with this view? Give reasons for your answer.

6 *Lenin's foreign policy*

One foreign policy or two?

Key points

- During the Civil War, Lenin promoted world revolution, seeing it as a key to the survival of Bolshevism in Russia
- Comintern (Communist International) was established in 1919 to further the cause of world revolution but it was a failure
- Alongside their unsuccessful revolutionary foreign policy, the Bolsheviks operated a more successful orthodox foreign policy

World revolution

One of Lenin's chief priorities as Russia's head of government was the promotion of the cause of Communist revolution in other countries. The importance he attached to this cause showed itself in a number of ways, and he devoted a considerable amount of his own time and energy to it. He sent abroad to work as Bolshevik agents a number of talented organisers who could otherwise have been very usefully employed at home. Among them were Karl Radek, Maxim Litvinov and Y.A. Berzin, who were posted respectively to Germany, Britain and Switzerland. Another indicator of the high priority given by Lenin to the cause of world revolution was his readiness to dig deep into Russia's limited cash reserves in order to finance it. 'Do not stint at spending millions for agitation among the French and English', he instructed one of his agents abroad in 1918.

There were two main reasons why Lenin was so preoccupied with bringing about revolutions abroad:

- Lenin and the Bolsheviks were committed as a matter of principle to the overthrow of capitalism, not only in Russia but throughout the world. In place of capitalist empires and nation-states, they hoped to see the emergence of a world-wide federation of Soviet republics. Immediately after 1918, it appeared to Bolsheviks that there was a real opportunity to turn this dream into a reality. This was because post-war economic difficulties led to an upsurge in left-wing militancy across the whole of Europe.

- During the Civil War era, Lenin believed that the future of the Bolshevik regime in Russia was uncertain unless Communist revolutions took place in the industrialised countries of Western Europe. This belief arose out of Marxist assumptions about the political outlook of different social classes. Marxists, Lenin included, assumed that the urban working classes, or proletariat, were natural or instinctive socialists, whereas peasants, wedded to ideas of private property, were not. This gave rise to the further assumption that the position of a Communist government in an industrialised country with a large proletariat would be extremely secure (because its power base would be wide), whereas a similar government in a peasant country was unlikely to be viable (because its power base would be narrow). Lenin looked forward to Communist governments taking power in Western Europe because he thought that such governments would be solidly based and strong enough to prop up his own embattled and insecure regime in peasant Russia. What he was desperate for above all was a successful revolution in Germany, continental Europe's most advanced industrial country. He told the Seventh Communist Party Congress in 1918: 'It is the absolute truth that without a German revolution we are doomed.'

Comintern

Bolshevik tactics for promoting the cause of revolution in foreign countries involved working through local Communist parties. In 1918–19 these tactics were employed in piecemeal fashion in Germany, Austria and Hungary.

In March 1919 though, a new body was set up to co-ordinate the activities of Communist parties outside Russia. This was the Communist International, or Comintern. Grigory Zinoviev, one of Lenin's chief lieutenants, was appointed its chairman. Its staff included Karl Radek and Angelica Bablanoff, a Russian-born Marxist who before 1914 had been active in the affairs of the Italian Socialist party.

Comintern's aims were laid down in 1920 at its Second Congress, attended by sizeable delegations from Germany, Italy and France:

'It is the aim of the Communist International to fight by all available means, including armed struggle, for the overthrow of the international bourgeoisie and for the creation of an international Soviet republic as a transitional stage to the complete abolition of the state.'

To outward appearances, Comintern was a free and equal partnership of the Communist parties of different nations. Appearances were misleading. In practice, Comintern existed solely to further the interests of Soviet Russia. The Bolsheviks regarded their partners in Comintern as nothing more than pawns, and treated them as such. Foreign Communist parties were not given the scope to decide for themselves the political strategy they wished to pursue in their own countries. They were instead expected to adopt and to implement whatever line was decided upon by their paymasters in Moscow.

Initially Comintern had some successes. In March 1919, Hungary became a Soviet republic under Bela Kun. Soon afterwards, a Soviet republic was proclaimed in the German state of Bavaria. In Britain in 1920 a number of Marxist organisations came together to form the Communist Party of Great Britain. In France in the same year French Communists broke away from the socialists to form their own party. The Italian Communists followed suit in 1921.

However, these successes proved to be short-lived, and the boasts of Soviet propaganda (see p40, Figure 7) were made to look empty. The Bavarian republic was crushed in May 1919, Bela Kun was overthrown in August 1919 and in the 1920s the Communist parties of Western Europe attracted pitifully small support. After its initial flourish in 1919–21, Comintern went into a sharp decline. It was finally dissolved in 1943.

Figure 7
'Comrade Lenin clears the world of dirt': Soviet poster, 1920 (the dirt being kings, priests and capitalists)

Chicherin

After the Civil War, the Bolsheviks started to operate alongside their revolutionary foreign policy a more orthodox diplomacy which aimed at normalising relations between themselves and the capitalist countries. They did so in part because they recognised that they would have to live alongside the capitalist world for longer than they had previously hoped, and in part because they were anxious, as part of their efforts to revive the economy, to boost Russia's foreign trade. The main architect of this orthodox foreign policy was Georgi Chicherin (1872–1936), a Bolshevik of aristocratic origin who succeeded Trotsky as Commissar for Foreign Affairs in 1918 and held the post until 1930.

Chicherin's orthodox foreign policy was a good deal more successful than Comintern's revolutionary one. A number of useful agreements were made, notably with Germany. Soviet Russia made overtures to Germany in particular because the two states had several common interests:

◆ Both were outcast nations in the early post-war world: Germany as a result of its defeat, and Soviet Russia as a result of the Bolshevik revolution.

◆ Both were hostile to the re-created state of Poland, having lost territory to it (Germany lost territory to Poland under the 1919 Versailles treaty, Russia under the 1921 treaty of Riga).

◆ The treaty of Versailles imposed severe restrictions on Germany's armed forces. Germany wanted to get round these restrictions and saw the manufacture of weaponry by German firms based in Russia as a way of doing so. Russia stood to gain from such an arrangement because it would offer access to German economic expertise.

A secret Russo-German treaty relating to the manufacture of armaments by German companies on Russian soil was signed in March 1921. A year later, under the treaty of Rapallo (April 1922), Soviet Russia and Germany agreed to resume normal diplomatic relations, a step involving the exchange of ambassadors. Rapallo also opened the way to closer economic ties between the two countries.

An improvement also took place in the early 1920s in relations with Britain, Russia's most committed opponent during the period of Allied intervention. In 1921 an Anglo-Soviet agreement was signed in London, under which trade between the two countries was to be channelled through a Russian company, ARCOS (All-Russian Co-operative Society), operating in Britain. Full diplomatic relations between Britain and Soviet Russia were re-opened in 1924 when Ramsay MacDonald's Labour government came to power. By 1924, Soviet Russia had re-opened diplomatic relations with all major powers except the United States.

Soviet foreign policy in the Lenin era was to some extent self-contradictory. Comintern was trying to overthrow the governments of capitalist countries while Chicherin was trying to do business with them. The most glaring example of this contradiction occurred in March 1921. At the same time that L.B. Krasin, People's Commissar for Foreign Trade, was in Berlin negotiating the armaments manufacture agreement with the head of the German army, an abortive Comintern-backed uprising by German Communists was taking place in the Ruhr. 'Soviet Russia's right hand', observes M.V. Glenny (*The Soviet Union*, 1978), 'often did not appear to know what the left hand was doing'.

Studying Lenin's foreign policy

1 Write two paragraphs, explaining (i) the aims of Comintern's revolutionary foreign policy, and (ii) the aims of Chicherin's orthodox diplomacy.

2 Write a paragraph explaining why, during the Civil War era, Russia's Communist leaders saw foreign policy as an essential part of their strategy for survival at home rather than a distraction from it.

3 'Not an international organisation but an arm of the Soviet Communist Party'. To what extent, and for what reasons, would you agree with this judgement on Comintern?

4 Make notes summarising the ways in which Soviet Russia benefited from Chicherin's orthodox foreign policy.

7 Historical interpretations

Was Lenin the begetter of Stalinism?

Key points

◆ After Stalin's death, historians accused him of perverting Lenin's principles
◆ Right-wing Western historians such as Richard Pipes believe Stalinism grew directly out of Leninism
◆ Many Western historians do not accept Pipes' conclusions

When Lenin died in January 1924, he left behind a number of major unsolved problems. Prominent among them were the problems of 'bureaucratism' and economic strategy. Above all, though, there was the problem of the succession.

In his so-called 'political testament', drafted in December 1922, Lenin made it clear that he had reservations about all of his possible successors. Trotsky was guilty of 'an excess of self-confidence'. Stalin could not be trusted to wield power with 'sufficient caution'. The opposition of Kamenev and Zinoviev to the seizure of power in October 1917 was 'not an accident'. Bukharin's theoretical views could only be regarded as fully Marxist 'with great reserve'. In a postscript to the 'political testament', written in early 1923, Lenin described Stalin as disloyal, intolerant, discourteous and capricious, and called for his dismissal as Communist Party General Secretary. The 'political testament' left little doubt that Lenin wanted to be succeeded by a collective leadership and not by any one individual.

In the event, Lenin was succeeded by Stalin. Stalin, of course, went on to become one of the most bloodstained rulers of modern history. He waged war on the Soviet peasantry in the era of collectivisation, he forced through rapid industrialisation in the 1930s more or less regardless of its human cost, and he bore primary responsibility for the 'great terror' of the late 1930s. But at each point in his career, Stalin justified his decisions by reference to the words and actions of Lenin. He unfailingly projected himself as Lenin's disciple. Within Soviet Russia he was the chief promoter of the 'Lenin cult' which, among other things, saw Petrograd renamed Leningrad and Lenin's embalmed corpse put on public view in a mausoleum in Moscow's Red Square.

Lenin and Stalinism

Official Soviet interpretations

Stalin's political heirs within the USSR admitted he had been guilty of enormous crimes. The first of them to do so was Khrushchev in his famous 'secret speech' to the Twentieth Party Congress in 1956. The USSR's post-1953 Communist leaders were, however, all too aware that branding Stalin as a criminal raised awkward questions about the relationship between the ideas and policies of Stalin and those of Lenin. If it were accepted that Stalin had genuinely been inspired by Lenin's ideas and practices, it followed that these ideas and practices, and by extension Communist ideas in general, bore a substantial measure of responsibility for the atrocities committed in the 1930s and afterwards. This was a conclusion which Stalin's Communist successors could not accept. To have done so would have been tantamount to admitting that the entire Communist project in Russia had been a gigantic mistake. Official interpretations of Soviet Russia's history in the years after Stalin's death therefore tried to draw a sharp dividing line between Leninism and Stalinism.

The official line on the differences between Lenin and Stalin was first set out in Khrushchev's 'secret speech' of 1956. In this speech, Krushchev argued that Lenin, unlike Stalin, had been a true Marxist. Lenin, he maintained, had upheld democracy or 'collegiality' within the Communist Party and had opposed the cult of the individual, whereas Stalin had sought personal dictatorship and self-glorification. He further argued that Stalin had been a sadistic practitioner of mass terror, whereas Lenin had used 'severe methods' only against 'class enemies' and even then only in the most necessary cases.

This in essence remained the official interpretation until the collapse of the Soviet Union in 1991, though Mikhail Gorbachev put his own particular gloss on it in the late 1980s by comparing Stalin's 'rigid' centralisation-and-command economic system' unfavourably with the NEP, presumably because the latter was akin to his own policy of *perestroika*, or economic restructuring. A sarcastic but not unfair summary of official Communist interpretations of the differences between the Lenin and Stalin eras was offered in 1989 by the Russian historian Alexander Tsipko: 'Everything was all right, the road being taken was quite correct, but then came a bad man and distorted everything' (quoted in R. W. Davies, *Soviet History in the Yeltsin Era*, 1997).

Right-wing Western historians

The idea that the Russian revolution was on course but somehow took a wrong turn with Stalin has since 1956 been derided by right-wing historians in Britain and the United States. The most assertive of them maintain instead that Stalinism grew directly out of Leninism. Currently, the most authoritative exponent of this view is Richard Pipes, author of *The Russian Revolution 1899–1918* (1990) and *Russia Under the Bolshevik Regime 1919–1924* (1994). Pipes is a Polish-born Harvard professor and self-styled 'conservative anarchist' who in the early 1980s advised President Reagan on Soviet affairs. He writes in *Russia Under the Bolshevik Regime*:

'Every ingredient of what has become known as Stalinism save one – murdering fellow Communists – he [Stalin] had learned from Lenin, and that includes the two actions for which he is most severely condemned:

collectivisation and mass terror. Stalin's megalomania ... and his other odious personal qualities should not obscure the fact that his ideology and *modus operandi* were Lenin's. A man of meagre education, he had no other source of ideas.'

Pipes offers a number of arguments in support of this view that Lenin was the begetter of Stalinism:

◆ He argues that Lenin's theoretical views on the role of the Communist Party opened the way to Stalinism. The views in question arose out of Marx's assumption that between the overthrow of capitalism by revolution and the emergence of a socialist society, there would have to be a transitional period characterised by the 'dictatorship of the proletariat'. Lenin adapted Marx's teaching, and said that during this transitional period, dictatorial power would not be exercised by the proletariat as such but rather by an elite or 'vanguard' party – the Bolsheviks – acting on behalf of the proletariat. Lenin, says Pipes, committed the Bolsheviks to a doctrine that sanctioned the use of arbitrary and 'inhuman' methods, and by so doing corrupted his followers.

◆ He emphasises that Lenin not only preached violence, but as Soviet Russia's head of government practised it as well – in its most extreme forms. Colleagues who were squeamish about the use of terror were mocked. Lenin, argues Pipes, set a personal example of cruelty, and thus bears responsibility for the culture of brutality which grew up within the Communist ranks.

◆ He points out that the machinery of repression used by Stalin in the 1930s – the secret police, concentration camps and so on – had been put into place by Lenin before 1924. He dismisses the claim of Khrushchev and others that circumstances left Lenin with no alternative but to adopt repressive methods, pointing out, among other things, that the Cheka was formed before, not after, the emergence of organised opposition to the Bolsheviks. Lenin, he maintains, created an apparatus of terror not because he was forced to, but because he was a totalitarian dictator who believed that the Communist Party had the right 'to subject to itself all organised life without exception'.

◆ He stresses the strength of the personal ties between the two men. Stalin, he argues, was Lenin's protégé, rising to prominence in the Bolshevik ranks as a result of Lenin's sponsorship. He plays down the importance of the breakdown in relations which took place in 1922–23, suggesting that the shortcomings Lenin attributed to Stalin in his political testament were 'not very serious'.

Richard Pipes' views on the relationship between Lenin and Stalin have been echoed not only by other right-wing Western historians, but also by Soviet dissident writers such as Alexander Solzhenitsyn (*The Gulag Archipelago*, 1973) and by post-Soviet Russian historians like Dmitri Volkogonov. In his biography of Lenin, published in 1994, Volkogonov is as scathing as Richard Pipes: 'Everything done in Soviet Russia after Lenin's death was done according to his blueprint, his precepts, his principles.'

Liberal Western historians

There are many Western historians who, though neither blind to Lenin's cruelty nor admirers of Soviet Communism, reject the views of Pipes and Volkogonov. They include Stephen Cohen, Bukharin's biographer, and British scholars such as Robert Service, Edward Acton and the late Alec Nove. These historians do not endorse Khrushchev's view that Stalinism was simply an aberration but, on the other hand, argue that it is an over-simplification to think in terms of a straight line between Lenin and Stalinism. They see continuities between Lenin and Stalin, but they also see discontinuities. The most important of these discontinuities are set out below. Note, though, that the historians named above would not necessarily endorse each of these points:

◆ Lenin may have been ruthless, but unlike Stalin he had ideals which he never fully abandoned. He was, for example, genuinely worried at the end of his life by the excessive power of the Communist Party bureaucracy, and was sincere in his wish to curb it.

◆ The quarrel between Lenin and Stalin in 1922–23 was not a petty squabble but a fundamental breach. Lenin belatedly recognised Stalin's true nature and the extent of his ambitions, and tried to stop him.

◆ Lenin was committed to one-party rule but, unlike Stalin, did not (and did not seek to) exercise a personal dictatorship.

◆ Lenin and Stalin employed terror as a political weapon in very different circumstances: Lenin resorted to terror when the Bolshevik regime was fighting for survival, but at the time of Stalin's purges there was no major internal threat to the regime.

◆ The scale of Stalin's atrocities went beyond anything Lenin ever contemplated.

Further Reading

Richard Pipes' views are most accessible in A *Concise History of the Russian Revolution* (1995), which is a condensed version of his two books covering the period 1899–1924, *The Russian Revolution 1899–1919* (1990) and *Russia under the Bolshevik Regime 1919–1924* (1994). Pipes' view of a straight line between Lenin and Stalinism is echoed in Dmitri Volkogonov, *Lenin: Life and Legacy* (1994). Introductory works which incorporate a more balanced view of the relationship between Lenin and Stalin include Robert Service, *The Russian Revolution 1900–1927* (second edition, 1991), Sheila Fitzpatrick, *The Russian Revolution 1917–1932* (second edition, 1994), and Alec Nove, *Stalinism* (Historical Association pamphlet, 1987). Much longer, but rewarding, are Orlando Figes, A *People's Tragedy: The Russian Revolution 1891–1924* (1996) and Robert Service, A *History of Twentieth Century Russia* (1997). Edward Acton, *Rethinking the Russian Revolution* (1990) analyses the historiography of the Russian Revolution and R.W. Davies, *Soviet History in the Yeltsin Era* (1997) includes a discussion of recent work by post-Soviet Russian historians on Lenin. The full text of Khrushchev's 1956 'secret speech' can be found in E. Crankshaw (editor), *Khrushchev Remembers* (paperback edition, 1971). A useful starting-point for Lenin's life and political thought is R. Appignanesi and O. Zarate, *Lenin for Beginners* (1994).

Lenin's principal Bolshevik lieutenants

Bukharin, Nikolai (1888–1938). Youngest of the top echelon of Bolshevik leaders under Lenin and one of the few not to use a pseudonym. The son of two Moscow schoolteachers. Member of the Bolshevik Central Committee (from 1917 onwards) and of the Politburo (from 1920). Editor of *Pravda* (1918–29) and author of numerous books on political and economic theory. Bukharin was a cultivated man and essentially a thinker rather than a doer. The political course he followed during 1917–24 was erratic and raised questions about his judgement: in 1917 he was in Bolshevik terms a left-winger, opposing the Brest–Litovsk treaty, but after 1921 he became an extreme right-winger, supporting the NEP and calling on the Soviet peasantry to enrich itself. Executed in 1938 after the third of Stalin's 'show trials'.

Dzerzhinsky, Felix (1877–1926). Born into a Polish landed gentry family. Head of the Cheka (1917–22) and of its successor organisations, the GPU and OGPU. He also served as People's Commissar for Internal Affairs (1919–22) and People's Commissar for Transport (1921–24), and was a member of the Orgburo (see pXX, Figure 5) and the Bolshevik Central Committee (from 1917). Lenin valued Dzerzhinsky because of his loyalty, fanaticism and administrative ability, but he did not hold him in much regard as a thinker or policy-maker. Never served on the Politburo under Lenin. Died of a heart attack aged 49.

Kamenev, Lev (1883–1936). Born in Moscow, the son of a railway engineer. Real name Rosenfeld. A member of the Politburo (1919–25), the Bolshevik Central Committee (from 1917) and chairman of the Moscow soviet (1919–26) (note that Moscow became Russia's capital in March 1918). Also served as Deputy Chairman of Sovnarkom (1922–24). Kamenev was a moderate in Bolshevik terms, opposing Lenin's April Theses, arguing in October 1917 that the proposed seizure of power was premature, and protesting against Cheka excesses during the Civil War. His humane and decent instincts (which he did not always act upon) were viewed by the hard men in the Bolshevik ranks as evidence of weakness. He was, however, on closer personal terms with Lenin than any of the other Bolshevik leaders, and was editor of Lenin's *Collected Works*. Executed in 1936 following the first of Stalin's 'show trials'.

Stalin, Josef (1879–1953). A Georgian of peasant origins, his real name was Djugashvili. Stalin was a pseudonym meaning 'man of steel'. After 1917 the key figure in the Communist Party bureaucracy, serving on the Central Committee (from 1917 onwards), the Politburo (from 1919) and the Orgburo (also from 1919). Became Communist Party General Secretary in 1922. Was also People's Commissar for Nationalities (1917–23) and head of the Rabkrin, or Workers' and Peasants' Inspectorate (1922–24), an organisation set up by the Bolsheviks to root out disloyal officials from the civil service. Stalin had neither the intellect of Bukharin or Kamenev nor the panache of Trotsky or Zinoviev, and tended to be regarded by his colleagues (among whom he was referred to as 'Comrade Card Index') as an efficient but unimaginative administrator. In practice, he was building up the immensely strong power base within the Party bureaucracy during the Lenin era which enabled him to out-manoeuvre Lenin's other lieutenants in the power struggles of the 1920s and to establish himself as a dictator. Paranoiac and a megalomaniac.

Trotsky, Leon (1879–1940) Born, like Zinoviev, into a landowning family in the Ukraine. His real name was Bronstein: Trotsky was a pseudonym taken from the name of one of his gaolers in the 1900s. People's Commissar for Foreign Affairs (1917–18), Commissar for War (1918–24), Commissar for Transport (1920) and member of the Politburo from 1919 onwards. For all his ability and dynamism, Trotsky was not a popular figure within the Bolshevik ranks. His aloofness, impatience and arrogance gave offence. In addition, as Commissar for War he offended the 'military' Bolsheviks, who disliked reliance on ex-Tsarist officers and trades unionists and who opposed his plans in the later stages of the Civil War to impose military discipline on the industrial workforce. Nor were Trotsky's Menshevik past or his Jewish origins forgotten (anti-semitism was widespread in the fast-growing Communist Party of the Civil War era). Trotsky was ill-suited to the political in-fighting which went on after Lenin's death. He was stripped of his responsibilities in the mid-1920s and exiled in 1929. Murdered by a Stalinist agent in Mexico in 1940.

Zinoviev, Grigory (1883–1936). Born into a family of small-scale landowners in the Ukraine. Real name was Radomysylsky. Chairman of the Petrograd soviet (1917–26) and of Comintern (1919–26). Served on the Politburo from 1919 onwards and also on the Bolshevik Central Committee. Zinoviev was a powerful orator but not, according to Trotsky, very much else. Zinoviev was ambitious, coarse and blustering, and was prone to lose his nerve under pressure. Orlando Figes (*A People's Tragedy*) calls him 'a coward and an opportunist'. Executed with Kamenev in 1936.

Table 1

Economic recovery under the NEP (base: 1913 = 100)

These figures do not show the actual amounts of coal, steel etc. produced. What they show is production in different sectors of the economy in each of the years 1920–26 expressed as a proportion of the 1913 level, with 1913 production being expressed in the form of base of 100. This allows:

◆ comparison to be made between production in any one sector of the economy under the NEP and pre-war levels of production in the same sector.

◆ some comparison to be made between the performance of different sectors of the economy under the NEP.

	1920	**1921**	**1922**	**1923**	**1924**	**1925**	**1926**
Industrial production (by value)	14	20	26	39	46	76	108
Coal production (tonnage)	30	31	33	47	56	62	95
Electricity production (kilowatt hrs)	na*	27	40	59	80	150	180
Iron production (tonnage)	na	3	5	7	18	36	58
Steel production (tonnage)	na	4	9	17	27	51	74
Grain production (tonnage)	58	47	63	71	64	91	96
Rail freight carried (tonnage)	na	30	30	44	51	63	na

*na = not available

Figures taken from A.Nove, *An Economic History of the USSR* (1986)

Table 2

Fluctuations in the membership of the Communist Party, 1917–24

Number of party members in thousands

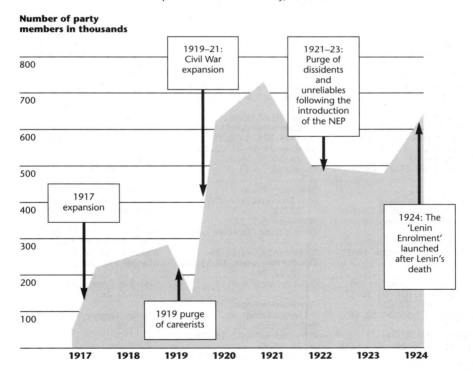

PER snack | 65 2.5 3.5 chicken satay snacks

Prep: **10** minutes   Cook: **10** minutes

These mini chicken kebabs with a satay dip can be served as a light lunch or supper dish with a selection of green vegetables or salad. Alternatively, they make great party food – hand them round at drinks parties or a festive bash.

225 g/8 oz skinned, boned chicken breast fillets
3 tablespoons very low-fat plain yogurt
1 teaspoon finely chopped fresh root ginger
pinch of ground turmeric
pinch of ground coriander
pinch of ground cumin
salt and freshly ground black pepper
¼ cucumber, cut into thin strips
2 spring onions, cut into strips

Satay sauce:
2 level tablespoons peanut butter
squeeze of lemon juice
½ teaspoon curry paste
2–3 tablespoons very low-fat natural fromage frais

1 Cut the chicken into strips and place in a bowl with the yogurt, ginger, ground spices and seasoning. Stir well to coat the chicken strips with the spicy mixture.

2 Thread the chicken onto 8 mini kebab skewers and then cook them under a preheated very hot grill for about 10 minutes, turning them frequently, until the chicken is cooked right through.

3 Meanwhile, make the satay sauce by mixing all the ingredients together and blending gently until smooth.

4 Serve the chicken kebabs with the cucumber and spring onion strips, and dip into the satay sauce.

OR...

Make an alternative dip by mixing 200 g very low-fat natural fromage frais with 2 level teaspoons Thai red or green curry paste (50 cals, 2 Checks, 0.5 g fat per snack), or some finely chopped red chilli and chopped fresh coriander leaves.

15 | 0.5 ① tricolore sticks

PER stick

Prep: 10 minutes

The distinctive Italian national flag is striped red, white and green, like these little snacks of low-fat mozzarella, basil leaves and cherry tomatoes. Quick and easy to assemble, you can keep them in the fridge to eat as a light bite, or serve them as party canapés.

8 cherry tomatoes
60 g/2 oz low-fat mozzarella
8 fresh basil leaves
oil-free French dressing for drizzling (optional)
sea salt and freshly ground black pepper

1 Halve the cherry tomatoes and cut the mozzarella into 8 cubes.

2 Thread half a cherry tomato on to a cocktail stick, followed by a cube of mozzarella and a basil leaf. Then add the remaining tomato half.

3 Repeat with the remaining ingredients until you have 8 tricolore sticks. Drizzle with oil-free dressing if wished and grind over a little sea salt and black pepper.

OR...

Ring the colour changes with yellow cherry tomatoes rather than the usual crimson ones.

35 | 1.5 ⓪⑤ italian cheesy stuffed tomatoes

SERVES two

Prep: **5** minutes

Although you can eat this snack all the year round, it is best during late summer when the tomatoes are fragrant and bursting with flavour. Always use tomatoes that are not too firm and have a characteristic tomato scent – those sold on the vine are very good.

2 medium ripe tomatoes
85 g /3 oz low-fat cottage cheese with chives
2 spring onions, chopped
½ sweet red pepper, de-seeded and finely chopped
salt and freshly ground black pepper
fresh chives to garnish

1 Slice the tomatoes in half horizontally. Scoop out the seeds with a teaspoon and discard.

2 Mix the cottage cheese with the chopped spring onions and red pepper. Season to taste with salt and pepper.

3 Spoon the mixture into the hollowed-out tomatoes and serve garnished with fresh chives.

OR...

Instead of cottage cheese, substitute the same quantity of very low-fat fromage frais (20 cals, 1 Check, 0.5 g fat per serving). If you don't have a red pepper, chop up some yellow or green instead. If wished, add some parsley, basil or mint.

loaded potato skins

Prep: **5** minutes plus cooking potatoes   Cook: **5** minutes

2 medium baking potatoes
30 g/1 oz half-fat Cheddar cheese, grated
2 spring onions, finely chopped
2 cherry tomatoes, chopped
salt and freshly ground black pepper

1 Scrub the baking potatoes and either cook them in the microwave or bake in a preheated oven at 200°C, 400°F, Gas Mark 6 for about 1 hour until tender.

2 Slice the potatoes in half lengthways and, with a small spoon, scoop out the flesh, just leaving a thin layer of potato inside the outer skin.

3 Mix the grated Cheddar cheese with the chopped spring onions and tomatoes, and season to taste with salt and freshly ground black pepper. Pile the mixture into the hollowed-out potato skins.

4 Pop the loaded potato skins under a preheated hot grill for about 5 minutes until they are bubbling and golden brown on top. Serve immediately.

OR...

1 Fill the potato skins with some very low-fat fromage frais or cottage cheese mixed with chopped grilled peppers and fresh herbs (100 cals, 4 Checks, 0.5 g fat per serving).

2 Fill each potato skin with a tablespoonful of fresh tomato salsa, sprinkle with the grated half-fat Cheddar cheese, then place on a grill pan under a preheated hot grill until melted and bubbling (100 cals, 4 Checks, 2 g fat per serving).

You can fill scooped-out jacket potatoes with a wide variety of no-Check or low-Check toppings. Eat them as a snack or a main meal with fresh salad tossed in some oil-free French dressing. And don't just throw away the scooped-out potato: you can mash it for the children's tea, or mix with some flaked cod or haddock and fresh herbs and shape into a couple of fish cakes for freezing until required.

hummus with grilled vegetables

SERVES two **230** **9** **11**

Prep: **10** minutes   Cook: **5–10** minutes

If you don't want to be bothered to make your own low-fat hummus, you can cheat and buy a tub of ready-made from the supermarket. If so, make sure you check the calories and fat grams on the label. This is the sort of snack that can be made in advance and kept in the fridge for those occasions when you feel hungry and fancy a light bite. You can buy jars of tahini in most supermarkets and delicatessens.

225 g/8 oz canned chick peas, drained
1–2 tablespoons water
1 tablespoon tahini paste
juice of 1 lemon
2 garlic cloves, crushed
1 teaspoon olive oil
salt and freshly ground black pepper
pinch of paprika
sweet chilli sauce, to serve

Grilled vegetables:
Choose from the following:
1 red, yellow or green pepper, de-seeded and cubed
1 courgette, cut into chunks
1 red onion, quartered
2 firm tomatoes, halved
spray oil

1 Put the vegetables of your choice in a roasting pan and spray lightly with oil. Season with salt and pepper and place under a preheated hot grill for 5–10 minutes, turning occasionally, until they are softened and slightly charred. Alternatively, cook on a ridged cast iron grill pan.

2 Whizz the chick peas in a blender or food processor with the water, tahini paste, lemon juice, garlic and oil until you get a rough paste. Add more water or the can juices if necessary. Season with salt and pepper and transfer to a bowl.

3 Sprinkle the hummus with paprika and eat with the grilled vegetables and a dollop of chilli sauce.

OR...

1 You can serve the grilled vegetables with tsatziki made from 150 g very low-fat plain yogurt, lemon juice, diced cucumber, crushed garlic and lots of chopped mint (35 cals, 1.5 Checks, 0 g fat per serving).

2 Make a really fast dip by mixing 100 g very low-fat fromage frais with 1 teaspoon green pesto sauce (105 cals, 4 Checks, 6 g fat per serving).

3 In a real hurry, use vegetable crudités, e.g. raw carrots, celery, peppers and cucumber, instead of grilled vegetables.

SERVES two | 150 6 5 mexican spicy chicken wraps

Prep: **10** minutes

For a quick bite, stuff a mini tortilla wrap with a delicious filling of spiced chicken, tomato salsa and crisp salad – quick and delicious!

2 teaspoons low-fat mayonnaise

good pinch of curry powder

2 mini tortilla wraps, or 1 large cut in half

crisp lettuce leaves, torn

2.5 cm/1 in chunk cucumber, diced

1 x 115 g/4 oz cooked boneless chicken breast, skin removed

2 teaspoons tomato salsa

a few fresh coriander leaves, chopped

1 Blend the mayonnaise and curry powder together in a small bowl and spread over one side of each tortilla wrap. Pile some lettuce and cucumber on top.

2 Cut the chicken in shreds and pile on top of the salad, then add the tomato salsa and scatter with coriander.

3 Roll up the tortilla wraps tightly – and enjoy.

OR...

Fill the tortilla wraps with some grilled mixed vegetables and 2 teaspoons low-fat guacamole, which will give you 90 cals, 4 Checks, 3.5 g fat.

SERVES one | 85 3.5 7 eggy veggie dippers

Prep: **2** minutes   Cook: **3–6** minutes

This quick snack will take you back to your childhood when you ate your boiled egg with toasted 'soldiers'. However, for a much healthier, slimming and more tasty alternative, treat yourself to some steamed vegetable dippers instead.

1 large free-range egg

salt and freshly ground black pepper

Dippers:
Choose from the following vegetables:

2 broccoli florets

2 cauliflower florets

8 thin green beans

4 baby asparagus spears

2 baby courgettes

1 Fill 2 small saucepans with water and bring to the boil. With a large spoon, carefully slide the egg into one pan and cook for about 3–6 minutes, depending on how firm or runny you like your eggs.

2 Add a pinch of salt to the other saucepan together with the vegetables of your choice, and boil, uncovered, for 4–5 minutes until just tender. Drain well.

3 Remove the egg from the pan and place in an eggcup. Slice off the top and serve with the hot vegetable dippers, seasoning with salt and pepper if wished.

OR...

Poach the egg instead of boiling it, and dip the vegetables into the runny yolk.

scallop and mushroom brochettes

Prep: **10** minutes   Cook: **6** minutes

4 rashers thin lean back bacon, rind removed

225 g/8 oz scallops, preferably with corals

juice of ½ lemon

8 button mushrooms

salt and freshly ground black pepper

snipped chives, to garnish

Honey mustard dip:

85 g/3 oz very low-fat fromage frais

1 heaped teaspoon honey mustard

1 Remove any fat from the bacon and then cut each rasher in half. Lay the rashers flat on a board and stretch them out with the blade of a knife to make them thinner and more elongated.

2 Sprinkle the scallops with the lemon juice and wrap each one in a bacon rasher. Thread alternately with the button mushrooms onto 4 skewers.

3 Place the brochettes under a preheated hot grill and cook them for about 3 minutes each side, until the bacon is crisp, the scallops are cooked through and the mushrooms tender.

4 Meanwhile, in a small bowl, mix the fromage frais and honey mustard together until well blended. Serve as a dip with the hot scallop and mushroom brochettes.

OR...

1 Use cherry tomatoes instead of mushrooms to alternate with the scallops.

2 Substitute whole-grain mustard for the honey mustard in the dip, and grate in a little lemon zest.

3 This recipe also works well with firm chunks of monkfish wrapped in bacon rashers. This will give you 190 cals, 8 Checks, 7 g fat per serving.

Fresh scallops are best for this recipe but they are sometimes quite expensive and hard to find, so you can use frozen ones instead. Basically, the simpler that the scallops are cooked and served, the better they taste, but beware of overcooking them or they will lose their succulent sweetness and become rubbery. Buy thin bacon rashers, not the thick ones. Not only will they be lower in Checks but they will also be easier to wrap around the scallops.

SERVES			
two	**140**	**6**	**1**

grilled tiger prawns

Prep: **12** minutes   Cook: **4** minutes

Most supermarkets with a fresh fish counter now sell raw tiger prawns. If not, you can buy them frozen and then thaw them overnight in the refrigerator. They taste delicious, will cook in minutes, and make a very nutritious snack. Alternatively, you can serve them as a main course with salad or a selection of fresh vegetables.

225 g/8 oz raw tiger prawns, unshelled

85 ml/3 fl oz very low-fat plain yogurt

1 garlic clove, crushed

1 teaspoon grated fresh root ginger

pinch of hot chilli powder

juice of ½ lemon

1 large mango, peeled, stoned and cut into bite-sized pieces

lemon wedges, to serve

1 Remove the shells from the prawns, leaving just the small piece of shell covering the tail. Now cut each prawn in half lengthways to just above the tail and fan it out.

2 Mix together the yogurt, garlic, ginger, chilli powder and lemon juice. Add the shelled prawns and turn them in the spicy yogurt mixture until well coated.

3 Thread the coated prawns and mango pieces alternately on to 4 skewers and place them under a preheated hot grill for 2 minutes each side, or until the prawns turn pink. Eat hot with lemon wedges.

OR...

1 In summer, you can cook these prawn skewers over hot coals on an outdoor barbecue for a really authentic flavour.

2 Substitute limes for lemons, and try using papaya or fresh pineapple instead of mango.

10
minutes

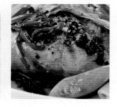

We know it seems incredible but you can prepare a delicious meal in only 10 minutes with the minimum of fuss. These recipes will make you want to rush into the kitchen when you come home from work and whip up some real fast food for supper.

Opposite: crab and herb tagliolini (recipe on page 29)

SERVES two | 220 | 9 | 2 | # stir-fried garlic chicken and couscous

Prep: **5** minutes   Cook: **5–7** minutes

For this quick recipe, you will have to buy a packet of the fast-cooking couscous – the type you just add to some boiling water, and then leave for 5–10 minutes, before forking through and fluffing up. This makes a really simple but satisfying meal, and children love it, too.

225 g/8 oz chicken breast fillets, skinned and cut into bite-sized pieces
spray oil
4 garlic cloves, crushed
salt and freshly ground black pepper
chopped fresh parsley, to garnish

Cherry tomato and lemon couscous:
60 g/2 oz quick couscous (dry weight)
4 cherry tomatoes, chopped
2 spring onions, chopped
juice of 1 lemon
salt and freshly ground black pepper

1 Put the couscous in a bowl and pour over an equal volume of boiling water, following the instructions on the packet. Set aside for about 5–10 minutes until the grains have absorbed all the water. Fork through and fluff up.

2 Meanwhile, cook the chicken pieces in a hot sauté pan or wok that has been sprayed lightly with oil. Cook over a high heat, turning the chicken frequently, until it is golden brown all over, about 4–5 minutes.

3 Add the crushed garlic and stir-fry for 1–2 minutes, until softened but not brown. Season with salt and plenty of ground black pepper and then sprinkle with parsley.

4 Stir the chopped tomatoes and spring onions into the couscous. Add the lemon juice and seasoning, and serve immediately with the hot garlic chicken.

OR...

1 Stir-fry the chicken as above but add some finely chopped chilli and grated root ginger instead of garlic for a more oriental flavour. Sprinkle with soy sauce just before serving with rice, not couscous.

2 Stir-fry the chicken and add a good pinch of ground cumin and ground coriander. Cook for 1 minute and then serve with the couscous and a little fiery harissa paste.

gingered hoisin chicken

SERVES two | 140 6 2

Prep: **5** minutes   Cook: **6** minutes

If the chicken is cut into small, bite-sized pieces, it will cook very quickly when tossed in a wok over a high heat. You can serve this quick and easy meal with a selection of fresh vegetables or just some plain boiled rice or noodles, but be sure to remember to add 100 cals, 4 Checks, 0.5 g fat, for each 30 g/1 oz dry weight or 75 g/2½ oz cooked weight boiled rice or pasta.

225 g/8 oz chicken breast fillets, skinned and cut into bite-sized pieces
1 tablespoon dark soy sauce
spray oil
2 garlic cloves, crushed
6 spring onions, sliced
115 g/4 oz broccoli florets, broken into smaller pieces
1 tablespoon hoisin sauce
salt and freshly ground black pepper
torn coriander leaves, to garnish

1 Put the chicken pieces in a bowl with the soy sauce and turn them over to coat thoroughly.

2 Heat a frying pan or wok over a high heat until it's very hot. Spray lightly with oil and then add the chicken pieces. Stir-fry for 2–3 minutes, turning the chicken often, until cooked and golden brown all over.

3 Add the crushed garlic, chopped spring onions and broccoli florets, and cook for a further 2 minutes, then stir in the hoisin sauce and warm through gently.

4 Season to taste with salt and pepper and serve, scattered with torn fresh coriander leaves.

OR...

1 You could use quartered or thickly sliced button or chestnut mushrooms or even some oriental shiitake ones instead of broccoli florets.

2 In the winter, shredded cabbage or spring greens make a delicious addition to this stir-fry.

3 Instead of hoisin sauce, use a small sachet of one of the ready-made stir-fry sauces available in supermarkets, such as ginger and spring onion flavour.

spicy 10-minute burgers

SERVES two | 180 | 7 | 7

Prep: **4** minutes   Cook: **6–10** minutes

225 g/8 oz less than 5% fat minced beef
½ onion, finely grated
1 teaspoon Worcestershire sauce
1 teaspoon Dijon mustard
1 egg, beaten
salt and freshly ground black pepper

1 Put all the ingredients in a bowl and mix well together until thoroughly blended. Alternatively, for a smoother texture, you can whizz them in a blender.

2 Divide the mixture into 2 equal-sized pieces and form each one, with your hands, into a burger shape.

3 Place the burgers under a preheated very hot grill and cook them for 3–5 minutes each side, depending on how well you like them done.

4 Serve with a crisp salad or, if you like to eat your burger in the traditional manner in a sesame seed burger bun with 1 tablespoon tomato ketchup and some lettuce, you will have to add on a whopping 170 cals, 7 Checks and 3 g fat.

If you try these real hamburgers made with 100 per cent minced beef, you will never yearn for one of the poor imitations from fast food outlets again. The better the quality of the meat, the faster the burgers cook and the better the flavour. If you can afford it, treat yourself and use very lean ground steak.

steak au poivre

SERVES two | 240 | 10 | 8

Prep: **2** minutes   Cook: **6–12** minutes

2 x 150 g/5 oz lean rump steaks, fat removed
spray oil
1 tablespoon black peppercorns
2 tablespoons red wine
2 tablespoons half-fat crème fraîche
1 tablespoon finely chopped parsley

1 Spray the rump steaks lightly with oil. Crush the peppercorns coarsely with a rolling pin or pestle and mortar, and sprinkle over the steaks, pressing them in lightly with your fingers.

2 Meanwhile, heat a ridged cast iron grill pan or non-stick frying pan until piping hot. Place the peppered steaks in the pan, pressing them down on to the hot surface with a spatula to sear them. Cook for 3–5 minutes each side, depending on how well done you like your steak. Remove from the pan and keep warm on 2 serving plates.

3 Add the red wine to the pan juices and let it bubble up for a minute or so, and then gently stir in the crème fraîche. Just warm through and then pour a little of this sauce around each steak. Sprinkle with chopped parsley and devour.

Use really lean steaks with all the visible fat removed. Rump is cheapest and has the most flavour, but fillet is leaner and more tender. You want a succulent steak which is juicy inside but browned outside – to do this, get the pan really hot before adding the meat.

caribbean pork and mango kebabs

SERVES two **250** **10** **7**

Prep: **5** minutes   Cook: **8** minutes

You will need really lean, tender pork for this recipe, and so it is worth splashing out on a little pork fillet or tenderloin. Some supermarkets now sell packs of diced pork, which will save you even more time.

juice of 1 orange
1 garlic clove, crushed
small piece of fresh root ginger, peeled and finely chopped
1 small red chilli, finely chopped
1 teaspoon runny honey
225 g/8 oz lean pork, cut into small cubes and fat removed
1 small mango, peeled, stoned and cubed
salt and freshly ground black pepper
fresh chopped mint, to garnish

1 In a bowl, mix together the orange juice, garlic, ginger, chilli and honey. Add the pork cubes and turn them over gently in the marinade mixture.

2 Thread the marinated pork and mango cubes alternately onto kebab skewers. Grind some salt and pepper over them and place on a grill pan.

3 Cook the pork kebabs under a preheated hot grill for 4 minutes each side until the pork is cooked through and golden brown, basting frequently with the leftover marinade mixture to keep them moist.

4 Sprinkle with chopped mint and serve immediately with a crisp salad.

OR...

1 These kebabs are even more delicious if you cook them outside on a barbecue over glowing hot coals.

2 You could substitute chicken for the pork, and fresh peeled pineapple chunks instead of mango. This is even more slimming and you can count just 200 cals, 8 Checks and 2 g fat per serving.

150 6 9 sausage and bacon brochettes

SERVES two

Prep: **5** minutes   Cook: **6–8** minutes

Now that you can buy low-fat sausages, you can continue to enjoy them as part of your new healthy, slimming regime. They are relatively cheap as well as being quick and easy to cook. This recipe gives you a mixed grill on a stick! Serve with steamed green vegetables or, in winter, some spicy red cabbage.

- 2 rashers lean back bacon, fat removed
- 4 low-fat chipolata sausages
- 8 button mushrooms
- 8 cherry tomatoes
- 4 bay leaves

1 On a chopping board, stretch out each bacon rasher thinly, pushing it away from you with the blade of a knife. Cut each rasher in half.

2 Cut the chipolata sausages in half and wind a bacon rasher around 4 of them.

3 Thread the bacon-wrapped sausages, button mushrooms and cherry tomatoes with the unwrapped sausages and bay leaves on to 4 kebab skewers.

4 Place the sausage kebabs under a preheated really hot grill, and cook for about 6–8 minutes, turning frequently, until the sausages are cooked through and browned.

5 Serve the kebabs immediately with some hot mustard or tomato ketchup and lots of green vegetables.

OR...

1 If wished, you could swap two of the chipolatas for 6 pitted prunes and wrap the bacon round these. This will give you 150 cals, 6 Checks and 6 g fat per serving, making the recipe lower in fat.

2 To make the kebabs more substantial and colourful, thread on some extra vegetables, such as chunks of red, green or yellow pepper, courgettes and aubergine.

grilled mackerel with mustard sauce

SERVES **two** | **300** | **12** | **19**

Prep: **2** minutes   Cook: **9–10** minutes

2 x 175 g/6 oz mackerel, cleaned
juice of 1 lemon
salt and freshly ground
2 tablespoons chopped parsley

Mustard sauce:
85 g/3 oz very low-fat fromage frais
1 tablespoon whole-grain mustard
1 level teaspoon reduced-fat mayonnaise
squeeze of lemon juice

1 Place the whole mackerel on the grill pan and squeeze some of the lemon juice over them. Season with salt and pepper, and cook under a high heat for 4–5 minutes. Turn the fish over and cook the other side for 4–5 minutes.

2 While the fish are cooking, make the mustard sauce. Mix the fromage frais with the whole-grain mustard and mayonnaise and stir in a squeeze of lemon juice.

3 Pour the remaining lemon juice over the cooked mackerel and sprinkle with chopped parsley. Serve with the mustard sauce.

A small mackerel will cook quickly – four to five minutes each side is enough to slightly char the skin and make the flesh sweet-tasting. Make sure that it is properly cleaned; all you need do is rinse the fish under running cold water before grilling.

smoked salmon scrambled eggs

SERVES **two** | **215** | **9** | **15**

Prep: **3** minutes   Cook: **3** minutes

4 large free-range eggs
2 tablespoons snipped chives
freshly ground black pepper
60 g/2 oz smoked salmon, finely chopped
spray oil

1 Break the eggs into a large bowl and beat well with a balloon wire whisk until the whites and yolks are thoroughly combined.

2 Add the snipped chives, a good grinding of black pepper (but no salt as the smoked salmon is quite salty) and beat lightly. Stir in the smoked salmon pieces.

3 Lightly spray a small saucepan with oil and place over a medium heat. Add the beaten egg mixture, then reduce the heat to a simmer and stir gently until the eggs scramble and set. Do not overcook or the mixture will become watery.

4 Remove the pan from the heat and divide the scrambled egg mixture between 2 warm serving plates. Eat immediately with grilled tomatoes and mushrooms, if wished.

We all know about scrambled eggs and how comforting they are, but have you thought of tarting them up and serving them with smoked salmon? Posh nosh, but a little smoked salmon goes a long way or you can use the cheaper trimmings, which are now available in many supermarkets.

barbecued salad with shrimp

SERVES **two** | **70** **3** **05**

Prep: **10** minutes   Cook: **7** minutes

This may sound quite bizarre but it is a brilliantly coloured salad with a distinctive smoky flavour. The salad leaves and vegetables are seared quickly on a hot grill with the prawns, then tossed in an oil-free dressing and eaten warm. It is typical of the healthy and innovative style of Californian cooking.

115 g/4 oz thin asparagus spears, trimmed

1 red pepper, de-seeded and cut into strips

1 yellow pepper, de-seeded and cut into strips

4 spring onions, trimmed

spray oil

1 small radicchio or chicory, trimmed and cut into wedges

175 g/6 oz raw tiger prawns, shelled

115 g/4 oz baby spinach leaves

salt and freshly ground black pepper

Dressing:

2–3 tablespoons oil-free vinaigrette

1 tablespoon light soy or teriyaki sauce

juice of ½ lemon or lime

1 Lightly spray the asparagus, peppers and spring onions with oil and place on a barbecue over hot coals or on a preheated ridged grill pan. Cook quickly, turning frequently, for 2 minutes.

2 Spray the radicchio or chicory and place on the grill, with the prawns, and cook for 2 minutes each side, until they turn pink. Toss the spinach leaves onto the grill for just long enough to warm and wilt them.

3 Mix all the dressing ingredients together, and gently toss the slightly charred barbecued salad vegetables and prawns in the dressing. Season to taste with salt and pepper and serve immediately whilst still warm.

OR...

1 Use thin slivers of skinned, boned chicken breast instead of prawns, and grill until cooked through and golden brown. This will give you 90 cals, 4 Checks and 1 g fat.

2 Sprinkle with chopped fresh herbs: basil, coriander, parsley and oregano are all delicious.

SERVES two | 190 8 9 smoked trout and melon salsa

Prep: **10** minutes

Fish and fruit sound an unlikely combination, but this one really does work. It's quick and easy to make for a light summer lunch, or it can even be served as an elegant first course when you are entertaining friends. To test whether a melon is ripe, press firmly on the ends with your thumbs – it should yield a little.

½ small ripe Cantaloupe or Charentais melon
1 teaspoon mixed peppercorns
2 spring onions, finely chopped
grated zest and juice of 1 lime
small bunch of fresh mint, chopped
225 g/8 oz smoked trout fillets
mint leaves, to garnish

1 Scoop out the seeds from the melon and discard them. Slice the melon in half and cut away the juicy flesh from the skin. Dice the flesh and place in a bowl.

2 Crush the mixed peppercorns lightly and add to the diced melon with the spring onions, lime zest and juice, and mint. Mix well together.

3 Arrange the melon salsa on 2 serving plates with the smoked trout fillets at the side. Alternatively, you can flake the trout flesh into bite-sized pieces and scatter it over the top of the melon salsa.

4 Garnish with mint leaves and serve, if wished, with a whole-grain roll or some crunchy brown rice.

OR...

1 Chopped mango or papaya flesh will make a delicious alternative if you are unable to buy a ripe melon.

2 For a more traditional meal, you can omit the melon and simply serve the smoked trout, sprinkled with lemon juice, with some hot horseradish sauce and very thinly cut wholemeal bread.

3 If you don't have a lime, a lemon will do!

crab and herb tagliolini

SERVES two | 370 | 15 | 1

Prep: **3** minutes   Cook: **8–10** minutes

175 g/6 oz tagliolini (dry weight)

spray oil

2 garlic cloves, crushed

grated zest and juice of 1 lemon

175 g/6 oz white crab meat, bits of shell removed

1 small red chilli, de-seeded and finely chopped

small bunch of fresh basil or coriander, chopped

salt and freshly ground black pepper

1 Cook the tagliolini in a large pan of boiling salted water, according to the packet instructions, until it is just tender but still a little firm when you bite into it (al dente, as the Italians say). Drain the cooked pasta through a colander, reserving a little of the cooking liquid for the sauce (about half a cupful).

2 While the pasta is cooking, lightly spray a small pan with oil. Place over a medium heat and sauté the crushed garlic for about 2 minutes until it is tender and releases its aroma – do not allow it to brown. Add the lemon zest and juice and cook for a further 1–2 minutes. Set aside.

3 Return the cooked, drained pasta to the pan with the reserved cooking liquid and, over a very low heat, heat through and toss gently with the crab meat, chilli, chopped herbs and the garlic and lemon mixture. All the strands of pasta should be gleaming and lightly coated.

4 Season to taste with some salt and pepper and serve immediately, sprinkled with more herbs if wished.

OR...

1 For a more concentrated, richer flavour, add 85 ml/3 fl oz dry white wine to the lemon and garlic and cook for a few minutes until it reduces a little. This tastes delicious but will add 30 cals, 1 Check, 0 g fat per serving.

2 If you don't have any tagliolini, you can substitute spaghetti, linguine or angel hair pasta. Even fettuccine or tagliatelle will work well in this dish.

If you like crab, you will love this unusual pasta dish. Obviously, it is best to use fresh crab if you can get it, but frozen is OK. However, canned crab is too watery for this dish with not enough texture or flavour, and therefore it will not do! Tagliolini is a very fine spaghetti-like pasta.

SERVES two 190 8 ⑪ spiced oriental salmon

Prep: **5** minutes   Cook: **6** minutes

Although salmon is an oily fish, it is still the slimmer's friend – highly nutritious and very filling, so you do not need to eat so much of it as white fish to feel satisfied. It is perfect for grilling and cooks very quickly. If you can find some wild salmon instead of farmed, buy it – it tastes much better.

2 x 100 g/3½ oz salmon fillets, skinned
1 tablespoon teriyaki sauce
½ teaspoon crushed mixed peppercorns
spray oil
2.5 cm/1 in piece fresh root ginger, peeled and shredded
1 small red chilli, de-seeded and shredded
1 tablespoon light soy sauce
torn fresh coriander leaves, to garnish

1 Place the salmon fillets in a bowl with the teriyaki sauce. Turn them over in the sauce to coat them lightly, then press the crushed peppercorns lightly into them.

2 Heat a ridged cast iron grill pan until it is very hot. Spray lightly with oil and then add the salmon fillets. Cook for about 3 minutes each side and then transfer to 2 warm serving plates.

3 Meanwhile, place the ginger, chilli and soy sauce in a small pan and heat through gently for 5 minutes until the ginger softens.

4 Pour the ginger mixture over the salmon and scatter with torn coriander leaves. Serve with pak choi or sugar snap peas.

OR...

1 If you don't have a ridged grill pan, you can cook the salmon fillets under a conventional hot grill, although you will not get the attractive striped effect.

2 Serve with a cooling raita made by stirring some diced cucumber, crushed garlic, finely chopped chilli and fresh coriander into a 150 g/5 oz pot very low-fat natural yogurt. This will give you 30 cals, 1 Check, 0 g fat per serving.

SERVES two | 185 7 13 poached egg and spinach salad

Prep: **2** minutes   Cook: **5** minutes

This warm salad of wilted spinach leaves and crispy bacon bits is topped with a softly poached egg. It is quick, easy and really delicious. Make it for supper when you dash in from work, or eat as a light lunch.

4 lean back bacon rashers, fat removed

2 large free-range eggs

225 g/8 oz baby spinach leaves

1 tablespoon oil-free vinaigrette dressing

salt and freshly ground black pepper

chives, to garnish

1 Grill the bacon rashers on both sides until they are really crisp and golden.

2 Meanwhile, poach the eggs, either in an egg poacher or by bringing a pan of water to the boil, then reducing the heat to a simmer and gently breaking the eggs into the hot water. Cover and simmer gently for 3–4 minutes until the whites are set.

3 While the eggs are poaching, put the spinach leaves in another pan, cover with a lid and cook gently over a low heat for about 2–3 minutes, shaking the pan occasionally, until the leaves wilt and turn bright green.

4 Remove and drain the spinach, pressing it down in a colander with a saucer to squeeze out all the liquid, and then divide the cooked spinach between 2 warm serving plates. Crumble the crisp bacon rashers over the top and drizzle with some vinaigrette. Season lightly with salt and pepper.

5 Carefully remove the cooked eggs from the poacher or slide them onto a large spoon out of the pan and place one on each plate, on top of the spinach and bacon. Garnish with chives and serve immediately.

OR...

1 If the spinach is really young and sweet, you need not cook it – just use the leaves raw.

2 Alternatively, you could use watercress or even peppery rocket leaves instead of spinach.

3 You could serve this dish with grilled tomatoes or field mushrooms. Cook them at the same time as the bacon.

penne with char-grilled cherry tomatoes

SERVES **two** 400 16 1

Prep: **3** minutes   Cook: **8–10** minutes

1 large aubergine, trimmed and cut into strips
225 g/8 oz cherry tomatoes
spray oil
225 g/8 oz penne (raw weight)
1 garlic clove, crushed
small bunch of parsley, chopped
salt and freshly ground black pepper

1 Lightly spray the aubergine slices and cherry tomatoes with the spray oil. Cook on a hot ridged cast-iron grill pan for about 5 minutes until tender and slightly charred, turning them occasionally to brown both sides. Alternatively, you can grill them under a conventional overhead grill.

2 Meanwhile, cook the penne in a large pan of salted boiling water until it is just tender but still retains a little 'bite' (al dente), for about 8–10 minutes. Drain in a colander and return the cooked pasta to the pan.

3 Gently mix in the grilled aubergine and cherry tomatoes, with the garlic and chopped parsley. Season to taste with salt and pepper and serve.

OR...

1 This dish works well with almost any pasta shapes – try spiral-shaped fusilli, conchiglie (shell pasta) or orecchiette (little ears). They all taste good.

2 If you don't like aubergine, you could use chopped peppers instead, or even some grilled mushrooms. Try a medley of wild and cultivated varieties.

3 Add some heat to the dish in the Sicilian manner with a de-seeded and chopped fresh red chilli – more if you like really spicy, hot food!

This is delicious served warm but you can prepare it ahead, store in a covered container and then eat it at room temperature as a pasta salad or picnic dish. Or take it to work with you as a packed lunch. Another option is to grate some Parmesan cheese over the top immediately before serving, but remember that just 1 level dessertspoonful will add 20 cals, 1 Check, 2 g fat.

20 minutes

You have even greater scope to create some exciting dishes in this chapter. The secret of cooking successful and delicious slimming meals is to use really fresh, good-quality ingredients. Here are some inspirational recipes for you to try... so get cooking!

Opposite: turkey saltimbocca (recipe on page 39)

75 ⬛3 ②2 chicken tom yum

SERVES **four**

Prep: **5** minutes   Cook: **10** minutes

This oriental soup is perfect as a light lunch or a warming supper dish. The name translates as 'spicy sour broth' and it tastes delicious. You can now buy all the ingredients in any supermarket, including the curry paste and tamarind. This recipe makes enough soup for 4 people, but you can allow it to cool and freeze 2 portions if you wish, or store in an airtight container in the fridge overnight.

2 teaspoons Thai red curry paste
225 g/8 oz chicken breast fillets, finely chopped
115 g/4 oz shiitake mushrooms, sliced
900 ml/1½ pints hot chicken stock
1 stick lemon grass, finely chopped
2.5 cm/1 in piece fresh root ginger, peeled and grated
3 teaspoons fresh tamarind
3 lime leaves (fresh or dried)
juice of 1 lime
3 spring onions, sliced
salt and freshly ground black pepper
torn coriander leaves, to garnish

1 Heat the curry paste in a large saucepan and cook gently for 1 minute over a medium heat. Add the chicken and mushrooms and stir until well coated with the paste.

2 Pour in the hot chicken stock and stir in the lemon grass, ginger, tamarind and lime leaves.

3 Bring the soup to the boil, and then reduce the heat to a bare simmer and cook gently for a further 5 minutes.

4 Stir in the lime juice and spring onions and pour the soup into serving bowls. Scatter some coriander over the top and serve hot.

OR...

Instead of chicken, use raw tiger prawns and substitute fish stock for chicken stock. Omit the mushrooms and curry paste and add a few drops of nam pla (Thai fish sauce) instead – you can buy this in your local supermarket. You will have a refreshingly clear seafood broth. Each serving will give you 75 cals, 3 Checks, 1 g fat.

SERVES two 185 7 ⑦ grilled chicken caesar salad

Prep: **10** minutes   Cook: **5** minutes

Many people find Caesar salad quite uninspiring, but adding char-grilled chicken will lift this dish into a class of its own. It's perfect for a light lunch on a warm summer's day.

- 2 x 115 g/4 oz boneless chicken breasts, skinned
- spray oil
- 3 tablespoons oil-free French dressing
- juice of 1 lemon
- 1 garlic clove, crushed
- 1 teaspoon Worcestershire sauce
- 1 raw free-range egg yolk
- salt and freshly ground black pepper
- 1 head cos lettuce, separated into leaves
- 2 level dessertspoons grated Parmesan cheese

1 Cut the chicken breasts into small pieces and cook on a hot griddle or ridged cast iron grill pan which has been sprayed lightly with oil for 4–5 minutes, turning them frequently, until they are cooked right through and appetizingly golden brown.

2 Mix together the French dressing, lemon juice, crushed garlic and Worcestershire sauce. Beat in the egg yolk and season with salt and pepper.

3 Toss the cos lettuce leaves in this dressing and divide between 2 serving plates. Arrange the grilled chicken pieces on top and sprinkle with grated Parmesan cheese.

SERVES two 255 10 ③ creamy spiced chicken with lentils

Prep: **5** minutes   Cook: **20** minutes

For speed, use canned, not dried, lentils for this dish. They are rich in fibre and protein, and extremely filling. If you serve this in the traditional manner with boiled rice, you must add on 100 cals, 4 Checks, 0.5 g fat for each 30 g/1 oz dry weight or 75 g/2½ oz cooked weight.

- 200 g/7 oz canned lentils, drained
- 1 teaspoon finely chopped fresh root ginger
- 1 teaspoon curry paste
- 2 tomatoes, skinned and chopped
- 2 spring onions, chopped
- 85 g/3 oz 0% fat Greek yogurt
- 2 x 115 g/4 oz skinned chicken breast fillets
- salt and freshly ground black pepper
- torn coriander leaves, to garnish

1 Put the lentils, ginger, curry paste, tomatoes and spring onions in a shallow pan. Stir well and heat through gently.

2 Add the yogurt, a tablespoonful at a time, stirring well between each addition.

3 Add the chicken, then cover the pan and cook gently over a low heat for about 20 minutes, turning the chicken halfway through. The chicken should be thoroughly cooked, not pink in the middle.

4 Check the seasoning and then serve immediately, sprinkled with fresh coriander.

OR...

Use Thai green curry paste instead of Indian, and add some chopped green pepper and baby carrots.

turkey saltimbocca

Prep: **5** minutes   Cook: **10** minutes

2 x 150 g/5 oz turkey breast steaks
2 wafer-thin slices Parma ham
2 large sage leaves
2 slices lemon
flour for dusting
2 teaspoons olive oil
115 ml/4 fl oz dry white wine
juice of ½ lemon
salt and freshly ground black pepper
2 tablespoons chopped fresh parsley

1 Carefully put each turkey breast steak between 2 sheets of greaseproof paper and then beat with a rolling pin (or your fist) until it is about 5 mm (¼ in) thick.

2 Place a slice of Parma ham on each steak, then a sage leaf and, finally, a slice of lemon. Fold over gently and secure with a cocktail stick to hold the shape. Dust very lightly with flour on both sides.

3 Heat the olive oil in a large non-stick frying pan, and add the folded-over turkey escalopes when it is hot. Sauté them for about 2–3 minutes on each side, until cooked and golden brown. Remove and keep warm.

4 Pour the white wine and lemon juice into the pan, and let it bubble away for 2–3 minutes until it reduces. Season to taste with a little salt and pepper.

5 Serve the turkey escalopes immediately with the pan juices poured over them, sprinkled with parsley. A selection of fresh boiled or steamed baby vegetables will make a delicious accompaniment to this dish.

OR...

1 You can use beaten out chicken breasts or proper veal escalopes instead of turkey steaks (280 cals, 11 Checks, 8 g fat per serving).

2 Instead of folding over the escalopes, you can secure them flat with a cocktail stick and then cook as above.

In classic Italian cuisine, this dish is always made with escalopes of veal, but it works equally well with turkey breast steaks, which are available from most supermarkets.

stir-fried lamb with noodles

SERVES **two** 370 15 8

Prep: **5** minutes   Cook: **12** minutes

115 g/4 oz Chinese egg noodles (dry weight)

spray oil

175 g/6 oz lean lamb leg or fillet, fat removed, cut into strips

2.5 cm/1 in piece fresh root ginger, peeled and chopped

2 garlic cloves, crushed

1 red pepper, de-seeded and thinly sliced

2 spring onions, sliced diagonally

225 g/8 oz shiitake or large field mushrooms, thinly sliced

1 tablespoon dark soy sauce

1 tablespoon hoi sin sauce

torn coriander leaves or flat-leaf parsley, to garnish

1 Cook the noodles in a large pan of boiling salted water for 4–5 minutes, until tender. Drain well in a colander.

2 Spray a wok or deep frying pan with oil and place over a high heat. When it is really hot, add the lamb strips and stir-fry for 2 minutes, until browned all over.

3 Add the ginger, garlic, red pepper, spring onions and mushrooms to the wok, and then continue stir-frying for about 2–3 minutes, until the pepper is bright and softened.

4 Stir in the soy and hoisin sauces, and add the drained egg noodles to the wok.

5 Toss the mixture gently until everything is lightly coated in the sauce.

6 Serve immediately, scattered with torn coriander leaves or parsley, with some stir-fried pak choi or winter greens tossed with garlic and ginger.

OR...

If you don't fancy lamb in this recipe, you can use the same quantity of chicken or pork instead. If so, you will have to count 330 cals, 13 Checks, 3 g fat for chicken; 330 cals, 13 Checks, 6 g fat for pork.

Ring the changes with some stir-fried lamb. Although this may sound unusual, lamb tastes fantastic cooked in this way, but you must use the leanest most tender cuts, such as the fillet, and slice it very thinly indeed.

SERVES two | 190 8 9 lamb tikka with crispy onions

Prep: **10** minutes   Cook: **10** minutes

Serve this fragrant dish with crunchy brown rice (100 cals, 4 Checks, 1 g fat per 75 g/2½ oz boiled) and a crisp green salad which has been tossed in oil-free vinaigrette.

85 g/3 oz very low-fat plain yogurt

1 tablespoon grated fresh ginger root

1½ teaspoons curry powder

225 g/8 oz lean lamb leg or fillet, fat removed, and cut into cubes

1 large red onion, thinly sliced into rounds

spray oil

salt and freshly ground black pepper

lemon wedges

1 In a bowl, blend together the yogurt, ginger and curry powder until well combined.

2 Season the lamb with salt and pepper and stir into the yogurt mixture. Set aside for 5 minutes.

3 Arrange the red onions in a 1 cm (½ in) thick layer in a foil-lined grill pan, season and spray lightly with oil.

4 Thread the lamb pieces onto wooden skewers and place on the grill pan beside the onions.

5 Cook under a preheated hot grill for 10 minutes, turning the lamb occasionally, until it is browned all over but still juicy and a little pink inside. The onions should be crisp and slightly charred. Serve with lemon wedges.

SERVES two | 150 6 4 thai spicy pork burgers

Prep: **5** minutes   Cook: **16** minutes

Serve these fragrant, fiery burgers with a fresh, crisp salad and cooling low-fat plain yogurt or hot chilli sauce. They make a delicious change from traditional beefburgers.

225 g/8 oz really lean pork, minced

1 small red onion, shredded

1 red chilli, de-seeded and finely chopped

1 garlic clove, crushed

1 stalk lemon grass, finely sliced

2 tablespoons finely chopped fresh coriander

salt and freshly ground black pepper

flour for dusting

1 Either mix the minced pork, red onion, chilli, garlic, lemon grass and coriander together in a bowl, or whizz briefly in a food processor until well combined. Season with salt and pepper.

2 With lightly floured hands, divide the mixture into 4 portions and shape into burgers.

3 Place the burgers under a preheated hot grill and cook for 8 minutes each side, until cooked through and golden brown.

OR...

To save time, spray the burgers lightly with oil and cook in a frying pan over a medium heat.

soy-fried pork with winter greens

SERVES **two** | **150** 6 5

Prep: **10** minutes   Cook: **10** minutes

225 g/8 oz boneless lean leg of pork, fat removed
1 tablespoon dry sherry
2 tablespoons dark soy sauce
1 teaspoon sesame oil
4 spring onions, chopped
2 sticks celery, chopped
½ small Savoy cabbage or winter greens, shredded
salt and freshly ground black pepper

1 Cut the pork into bite-sized chunks and place in a bowl with the sherry and 1 tablespoon soy sauce. Stir until the pork is well coated with the marinade mixture.

2 Heat the sesame oil in a wok or deep frying pan. When it is really smoking hot, add the pork in its marinade and cook briskly over a high heat, stirring all the time, for 2–3 minutes, until the meat is well-browned all over.

3 Add the spring onions, celery and cabbage, and stir-fry for about 5 minutes, until the pork is cooked and the cabbage or greens have turned bright green.

4 Add the remaining soy sauce and season to taste with salt and plenty of freshly ground black pepper. Serve immediately.

OR...

1 Use spray oil instead of sesame oil and save 20 cals, 1 Check, 2 g fat for each portion.

2 Strips of lean beef also work well in this dish. Buy tender rump or sirloin steak and remove all the fat before cooking. This gives 180 cals, 7 Checks, 7 g fat per serving.

When you rush home from work, you won't find an easier supper than this! Serve it with boiled rice or cooked Chinese egg noodles. Count an additional 100 cals, 4 Checks, 0.5 g fat per each 30 g/1 oz dry weight or 75 g/2½ oz cooked weight boiled rice or pasta.

SERVES two 150 6 6 thai crab cakes

Prep: **10** minutes   Cook: **6** minutes

Crab cakes are often made with mashed potato and then deep-fried, thereby piling on the calories. These spicy delicacies are relatively low in Checks and you can enjoy eating them without worrying about your waistline. Always use fresh crab meat if you can; its texture is firmer and less watery than frozen or canned crab meat, and it tastes better, too. You can use the creamy brown meat as well as the white for this recipe.

300 g/10 oz fresh crab meat
1 red chilli, de-seeded and chopped
3 spring onions, chopped
2 garlic cloves, crushed
large handful of fresh coriander leaves
2 teaspoons nam pla (Thai fish sauce)
1 tablespoon low-calorie mayonnaise
flour for dusting
spray oil

Dipping sauce:
2 tablespoons rice vinegar
1 rounded teaspoon sugar
1 teaspoon dark soy sauce
1 small red chilli, chopped
juice of ½ lime

1 Put the crab meat, chilli, spring onions, garlic, coriander leaves, nam pla and mayonnaise in a blender or food processor and blitz until you have a thick sludge.

2 Divide the mixture into 8 portions and shape with your hands into little patties. Dust very lightly with flour.

3 Spray a frying pan lightly with spray oil and place over a medium to high heat. When the pan is really hot, add the crab cakes and cook them for about 2–3 minutes each side, until golden brown. Be careful when you turn them over – make sure you use a spatula and do it very gently so as to keep their shape.

4 You can make the dipping sauce in advance, if wished. Just heat the rice vinegar and sugar in a small pan, stirring until dissolved. When it becomes syrupy, add the soy sauce, chilli and lime juice. Leave to cool.

5 Serve the crab cakes hot from the pan with the dipping sauce.

OR...

1 If you can get kaffir lime leaves, shred them into the crab mixture before blending for a citrusy flavour.

2 If you can't be bothered to make the dipping sauce, use bottled chilli sauce. The dipping sauce will keep in a screwtop jar in the fridge for 1 week.

herby tuna burgers

SERVES **two** | 210 | 8 | 1

Prep: **10** minutes   Cook: **6** minutes

You don't have to make fishcakes with fresh fish; you can use canned tuna instead. This is a nutritious and economical meal, and a good way of using up some leftover mashed potato – for example, if you've been making loaded potato skins.

225 g/8 oz boiled potatoes mashed with 2 tablespoons skimmed milk

175 g/6 oz canned tuna in brine or spring water, drained and flaked

3 spring onions, finely chopped

4 tablespoons finely chopped parsley

salt and freshly ground black pepper

flour for dusting

spray oil

lemon wedges, to serve

1 In a bowl, mix together the mashed potatoes, tuna, spring onions and parsley. Season to taste with salt and pepper.

2 Shape the mixture into patties, as large or as small as you like. Dust them very lightly with flour.

3 Spray a non-stick frying pan lightly with oil and, when it is hot, add the fishcakes. Cook for 2–3 minutes on each side, until golden brown.

4 Remove from the pan and squeeze some wedges of lemon over to serve.

cod and bacon wraps

SERVES **two** | 250 | 10 | 13

Prep: **5** minutes   Cook: **12** minutes

Even if you have forsaken fried cod in batter, you can still enjoy eating it in a low-Check way. Don't be put off by the combination of fish and bacon – they complement each other well. Take care not to overcook the cod or it will lose its succulence and will become dry.

225 g/8 oz cod fillets

4 x 15 g/½ oz rashers rindless streaky bacon

spray oil

2 large beefsteak tomatoes, halved

freshly ground black pepper

Creamy red pesto sauce:

85 g/3 oz virtually fat-free fromage frais

1 teaspoon reduced-fat mayonnaise

1 rounded teaspoon red pesto sauce

1 Cut the cod into 4 equal-sized portions. Stretch out each bacon rasher with the back of a knife, and wrap each piece of cod in a rasher.

2 Spray a non-stick baking pan with a little oil and place the cod and the halved tomatoes in the pan. Grind some black pepper over the top.

3 Cook in a preheated oven at 220°C/425°F/Gas Mark 7 for about 12 minutes, or until the cod is cooked and the bacon crisp.

4 While the cod is cooking, mix the fromage frais with the mayonnaise and red pesto. Serve with the cod and bacon wraps.

OR...

Monkfish is even firmer-fleshed than cod and works well in this recipe (235 cals, 9 Checks, 12 g fat per serving).

swordfish steaks with ginger and lemon

SERVES two | **150** | 6 | 6

Prep: **10** minutes   Cook: **6** minutes

2 x 150 g/5 oz swordfish steaks

2.5 cm/1 in piece fresh root ginger, peeled and grated

1 garlic clove, crushed

juice of 1/2 lemon

salt and freshly ground black pepper

spray oil

2 spring onions, thinly sliced or shredded

a few coriander leaves, shredded

lemon wedges to serve

1 Place the swordfish steaks in a shallow dish. Sprinkle over the ginger and garlic, and then squeeze over the lemon juice. Season with a little salt and pepper, and turn the fish steaks in the citrusy mixture. Set aside for 5 minutes to allow the flavours to develop.

2 Heat a ridged cast iron grill pan and spray lightly with oil. When it is really hot, add the marinated swordfish steaks and cook over a high heat for about 3 minutes each side, or until the fish is cooked through with an attractive striped effect on the outside. Pour any leftover citrus mixture over the top

3 Arrange the cooked swordfish steaks on 2 warm serving plates and scatter the shredded spring onions and coriander over them. Serve garnished with lemon wedges. Serve with assorted boiled or steamed fresh vegetables or a salad.

OR...

1 Use a freshly squeezed lime instead of a lemon for a more Caribbean flavour.

2 You can, if wished, substitute another firm-fleshed oily fish, such as fresh tuna or marlin steaks (175 cals, 7 Checks, 6 g fat per serving.

3 This tastes really good served with some fresh tomato salsa (available from most supermarkets). One heaped tablespoon salsa will add 10 cals, 0.5 Checks, 0 g fat.

Swordfish is rich in the essential omega-3 fatty acids which are particularly good for your health. However, current health advice recommends that pregnant women should avoid eating fresh swordfish, tuna or marlin. With its dense, meaty texture, swordfish is very filling and it will grill well without flaking.

SERVES two | 430 17 4 shrimp scampi with lemon linguine

Prep: **5** minutes Cook: **10** minutes

This popular seafood pasta dish was brought to the United States by Sicilian immigrants and is a fine example of healthy, unfussy Italian food. The original version uses a lot of olive oil, but this slimming variation is just as delicious. It is best made with raw tiger prawns; if you can't get fresh ones, use frozen and defrost before cooking.

175 g/6 oz linguine (dry weight)
1 teaspoon olive oil
2 garlic cloves, crushed
juice of 2 lemons
150 ml/¼ pint dry white wine
salt and freshly ground black pepper
225 g/8 oz raw tiger prawns, shelled
1 small bunch parsley, finely chopped

1 Bring a large pan of salted water to the boil and then add the linguine. Cook at a rolling boil for about 10 minutes until it is just tender but still retains some 'bite' (al dente). Drain well.

2 While the pasta is cooking, heat the olive oil in a large frying pan. Add the crushed garlic and cook for about 1–2 minutes until softened. Do not allow to brown.

3 Pour in the lemon juice and white wine and cook over a medium heat for about 5 minutes to concentrate the flavours and reduce the liquid a little.

4 Add the tiger prawns and cook for about 1 minute and then turn them – the cooked side should have turned pink. Cook for 1 minute on the other side. Do not leave for too long or the prawns will lose their tenderness and become tough.

5 Add the parsley and seasoning to taste, then fold in the drained linguine, tossing it gently in the lemony liquid so that all the strands are well coated. Divide between 2 serving plates.

OR...

You could use crab meat or even lobster if you are feeling adventurous. A cheaper alternative would be to substitute a packet of the frozen fruits de mer, which have been thoroughly defrosted. Add to the lemony sauce with their liquid for a more intense seafood flavour.

SERVES two 285 11 18 ham and cheese soufflé omelette

Prep: **10** minutes   Cook: **5** minutes

Eggs are rich in protein and can make a nourishing meal in minutes – even a large egg is only 3.5 Checks. Try to use organic free-range eggs when making omelettes; they have the best flavour, colour and texture when cooked. You can test whether an egg is fresh by placing it in a bowl of water: if it sinks, it's fresh.

3 large organic free-range eggs
3 tablespoons cold water
1 teaspoon Dijon mustard
salt and freshly ground black pepper
spray oil
60 g/2 oz half-fat Cheddar cheese, grated
100 g/3½ oz lean smoked ham, chopped
1 tablespoon chopped parsley

1 Separate the eggs into 2 clean, dry bowls. In one bowl, whisk the egg whites until they form soft peaks.

2 In the other bowl, beat the egg yolks and water until pale and creamy. Stir in the mustard and season lightly, then gently fold in the whisked egg whites with a metal spoon.

3 Heat a non-stick frying pan and spray with oil. When it is hot, pour in the egg mixture and cook gently over a low heat for a few minutes until the base of the omelette is set and golden.

4 Scatter the cheese and ham over the top of the omelette and place the pan under a hot grill until the top of the omelette is just set and the cheese melted.

5 Fold the omelette over and slide out of the pan. Divide in half and transfer to 2 warm serving plates. Sprinkle with parsley and serve with a crisp salad.

SERVES two 300 12 1 rainbow pasta

Prep: **10** minutes   Cook: **10** minutes

This colourful pasta dish is absolutely delicious and perfect for vegetarians. The pasta can cook while the vegetables are being grilled. If you prefer, you can roast the vegetables in a medium to hot oven.

4 baby courgettes, sliced
½ red pepper, de-seeded and cut into chunks
½ yellow pepper, de-seeded and cut into chunks
½ green pepper, de-seeded and cut into chunks
1 small red onion, quartered
4 cherry tomatoes
2 garlic cloves, halved
spray oil
175 g/6 oz fusilli (dry weight)
2 tomatoes, skinned and chopped
salt and ground black pepper
sprigs of thyme, to garnish

1 Prepare the vegetables and garlic and place all, except the chopped tomatoes, in a hot ridged cast iron grill pan which has been sprayed with oil. Cook over a medium to high heat, turning the vegetables frequently, for about 10 minutes, until softened and slightly charred. Do not allow them to burn.

2 Meanwhile, cook the fusilli in a large pan of boiling salted water for 8–10 minutes, or until it is just tender but retains some 'bite' (al dente). Drain well.

3 Transfer the fusilli and grilled vegetables to a large serving bowl. Add the chopped tomatoes and toss gently together. Season to taste with salt and pepper, and serve garnished with sprigs of thyme.

orecchiette with purple sprouting broccoli

SERVES two | 310 | 12 | 8

Prep: **5** minutes Cook: **10** minutes

150 g/5 oz orecchiette or other pasta shapes (dry weight)
225 g/8 oz purple sprouting broccoli, divided into florets
8 cherry tomatoes

Chilli dressing:
1 dessertspoon olive oil
juice of ½ lemon
1 small red chilli, de-seeded and finely chopped
salt and freshly ground black pepper

1 Cook the pasta in a large saucepan of boiling salted water for about 10 minutes, until it is just tender but still retains some 'bite' (al dente). Drain well in a colander.

2 Meanwhile, cook the broccoli in lightly salted boiling water for 3–4 minutes, and drain well. Grill the cherry tomatoes.

3 Whisk all the dressing ingredients together in a small bowl.

4 Lightly toss together the cooked pasta, broccoli and grilled cherry tomatoes, and then drizzle the dressing over the top.

OR...

Instead of tomatoes, toss the pasta and broccoli with crisply grilled and crumbled lean back bacon. Add 45 cals, 2 Checks, 3 g fat for each well-trimmed rasher.

Orecchiette are little pasta shapes (literally 'little ears') that are perfect for holding sauces and liquids. Here they are tossed with purple sprouting broccoli, a traditional British variety which you can buy from November to April, but you can use ordinary broccoli instead. This is reminiscent of the Roman way of cooking broccoli with chillies.

mughlai saag aloo

SERVES two | 130 | 5 | 2

Prep: **5** minutes Cook: **13** minutes

spray oil
1 onion, finely chopped
225 g/8 oz peeled potatoes, diced
1 red chilli, de-seeded and finely chopped
2 tablespoons garam masala
1 teaspoon black mustard seeds
150 ml/¼ pint hot vegetable stock
225 g/8 oz baby spinach leaves
salt and black pepper
115 g/4 oz very low-fat cottage cheese
finely chopped chilli, to garnish

1 Spray a large pan lightly with oil. Place over a medium heat and add the onion, potatoes, chilli, garam masala and mustard seeds. Cook for about 5 minutes, stirring frequently to prevent it sticking.

2 Add the hot stock and simmer for 5 minutes, then add the spinach. Continue cooking for 2–3 minutes until the spinach wilts and turns bright green. Season to taste with salt and pepper.

3 Spoon the mixture onto warmed plates and top each one with the cottage cheese and some chopped chilli.

The addition of cottage cheese transforms this Indian vegetarian dish into a main course. It's cheap, quick and easy to make – the perfect antidote to rich food.

herby smoked salmon frittata

SERVES **two** | 230 9 13

Prep: **10** minutes   Cook: **10** minutes

A frittata is an Italian omelette, which is finished off under the grill and then served either hot or at room temperature, cut into wedges. As well as making a good light lunch or supper dish, it is good finger food for packed lunches or picnics. You need not use top-quality smoked salmon for this dish – the trimmings will do just as well.

2 onions, thinly sliced
4 baby leeks, sliced
spray oil
3 large organic free-range eggs
2 tablespoons cold water
a few fresh chives, chopped
2 tablespoons chopped fresh dill
2 tablespoons chopped parsley
salt and freshly ground black pepper
100 g/3½ oz smoked salmon, chopped

Dill and cucumber sauce:
115 g/4 oz very low-fat fromage frais
¼ cucumber, finely diced
1 tablespoon finely chopped fresh dill
1 garlic clove, crushed
grated zest of 1 lemon
salt and freshly ground black pepper

1 Cook the onions and baby leeks gently until softened and golden in a large non-stick frying pan that has been lightly sprayed with oil.

2 Meanwhile, break the eggs into a large bowl, add the cold water and whisk until light and frothy and well combined. Stir in the chopped herbs, seasoning, smoked salmon and cooked onions and leeks.

3 Put the frying pan back on the heat and, when hot, pour in the frittata mixture. Cook over a low heat until the base is set and golden.

4 Pop the pan under a hot preheated grill to set and brown the top of the frittata. Slide out onto a serving plate.

5 While the frittata is cooking, mix together all the ingredients for the sauce.

6 Cut the frittata into wedges and serve with the sauce and a crisp dressed salad.

OR...

Make a vegetable frittata: sauté some chopped onions, courgettes, tomatoes and garlic, then stir into the egg mixture and cook as above. Sprinkle with 1 tablespoon grated Parmesan cheese before popping under the grill. This will give you 150 cals, 6 Checks, 12 g fat per serving.

30 minutes

You will find an international flavour to this 30-minute recipe collection. All the dishes are easy to make and, once you've done the preparation, many can be left to cook away while you relax. No matter how busy you are, there's still time to cook.

Opposite: sweet and sour chicken (recipe on page 58)

moroccan lemon chicken

SERVES two 180 7 5

Prep: **2** minutes   Cook: **25–30** minutes

Another recipe that is quickly prepared and then left to cook away while you relax with family or friends, or just sink down in front of the television after a hard day's work. Serve this with boiled wide noodles (pappardelle or fettuccine) at 100 cals, 4 Checks, 0.5 g fat per 75 g/2½ oz cooked portion (from 30 g/1 oz dry weight).

spray oil
2 x 150 g/5 oz boneless chicken breasts, skinned
10 black olives, pitted
200 ml/7 fl oz chicken stock
1 lemon, cut into slices
few sprigs of fresh oregano or thyme
2 tablespoons freshly chopped parsley
salt and freshly ground black pepper

1 Spray a sauté pan lightly with oil and, when it is hot, add the chicken breasts. Cook them for 4–5 minutes over a high heat, turning halfway through, until browned on both sides.

2 Add the olives, chicken stock, lemon slices and oregano or thyme. Cover the pan and simmer gently for about 15–20 minutes.

3 Uncover the pan and turn up the heat. Cook rapidly for 5 minutes, until the sauce thickens and reduces.

4 Stir in the parsley and season to taste with salt and pepper. Serve immediately.

OR...

1 Use a thinly sliced orange instead of a lemon for an equally citrusy but less sharp and more subtle flavour.

2 Serve with couscous in the North African style. Prepare according to the instructions on the packet and then count 200 cals, 8 Checks, 0.5 g fat per 150 g cooked serving (from 60 g/2 oz dry weight).

SERVES two | 170 7 2 sweet and sour chicken

Prep: **10** minutes   Cook: **12–15** minutes

You can make a slimming version of this classic Chinese dish by stir-frying lean chicken rather than deep-frying it in batter. Surprise yourself – it tastes even better than the traditional version.

spray oil
225 g/8 oz boneless chicken breast, skinned and cut into chunks
1 garlic clove, crushed
2 spring onions, sliced
1 red pepper, de-seeded and cut into chunks
1 pineapple ring canned in juice, chopped
salt and freshly ground black pepper

Sweet and sour sauce:
1 tablespoon light soy sauce
1 teaspoon white wine vinegar
2 teaspoons sweet sherry
1 teaspoon tomato paste
3 tablespoons fresh orange juice
1 level dessertspoon cornflour

1 Blend together all the ingredients for the sweet and sour sauce in a small bowl, taking care that the cornflour is thoroughly mixed in and that there are no lumps.

2 Spray a wok or frying pan with a little oil and place over a medium to high heat. Add the chicken chunks and stir-fry, turning all the time, for about 4–5 minutes, until the chicken is browned all over.

3 Add the garlic, spring onions and red pepper and continue stir-frying for 2–3 minutes, until just tender.

4 Add the chopped pineapple, and stir in the sweet and sour sauce. Reduce the heat and continue stirring until the sauce thickens and coats the chicken and vegetables.

5 Check the seasoning and serve immediately with boiled rice or egg noodles (100 cals, 4 Checks, 0.5 g fat for each 30 g/1 oz dry weight or 75 g/2½ oz cooked weight).

SERVES two | 225 9 8 duck with piquant mango sauce

Prep: **5** minutes   Cook: **20–30** minutes

Duck is so delicious yet rarely eaten by slimmers because the skin is so fatty. Here the skin is discarded and the rich meat is offset by a piquant fruit sauce. Serve with watercress tossed with fresh orange slices and an oil-free dressing.

2 x 150 g/5 oz duck breast fillets
1 medium ripe mango, peeled and stoned
juice of ½ lemon
1 tablespoon finely chopped fresh root ginger
1 red chilli, de-seeded and finely chopped
salt and freshly ground black pepper
1 tablespoon chopped fresh coriander

1 Cut some diagonal slashes in the skin of the duck breasts. Place them in an ovenproof dish and cook in a preheated oven at 200°C, 400°F, Gas Mark 6 for 20–30 minutes.

2 While the duck is cooking, cut half the mango into dice, and purée the rest with the lemon juice and ginger in a blender.

3 Put the mango purée in a pan with the diced mango and chilli, and heat gently over a low heat. Season to taste with salt and pepper and stir in the chopped coriander.

4 Remove the duck skin including the layer of fat underneath. Serve each duck breast surrounded by a pool of mango sauce.

speedy beef and ale stew

Prep: **5** minutes   Cook: **25** minutes

1 onion, thinly sliced

2 large carrots, thinly sliced

spray oil

225 g/8 oz lean beef sirloin, visible fat removed

2 teaspoons plain flour

150 ml/¼ pint beef stock

150 ml/¼ pint dark ale

1 teaspoon redcurrant or cranberry jelly

salt and freshly ground black pepper

1 tablespoon finely chopped parsley

1 Cook the onion and carrots over a medium heat for 5 minutes in a pan that has been sprayed lightly with oil.

2 Add the beef and cook, stirring occasionally, for 2 minutes, until browned all over.

3 Stir in the flour and then add the stock and ale, stirring all the time. Bring to the boil, then reduce the heat and add the redcurrant or cranberry jelly.

4 Cover with a lid and simmer for 15 minutes, until the beef and carrots are cooked and tender. Correct the seasoning and serve sprinkled with parsley. Cabbage, boiled but still crisp and sprinkled with black pepper, goes well with this stew.

In order to create this delicious stew within 30 minutes, you must use the best, most tender cut of beef that you can buy – beef sirloin is ideal. If you try to cheat and use a cheaper cut instead, the meat will be tough and stringy.

roast fillet of lamb with anchovies

Prep: **5** minutes   Cook: **20–25** minutes

250 g/9 oz lean fillet of lamb, fat removed

1 garlic clove, peeled and cut into slivers

3 drained anchovy fillets, cut into pieces

few sprigs of fresh mint

sea salt and pepper

spray oil

2 tablespoons chopped fresh mint

1 Place the lamb on a work surface and make a few small incisions with a sharp knife. Insert the garlic slivers, anchovy pieces and mint sprigs into these incisions and then grind some sea salt and black pepper over the top.

2 Lightly spray a small roasting pan with oil and place the lamb in the pan. Cook in a preheated oven at 200°C, 400°F, Gas Mark 6 for 20–25 minutes, depending on how pink or well done you like your lamb.

3 To serve, cut into thin slices, sprinkle with mint and add mint sauce, if wished. If you prefer mint jelly, add an extra 15 cals, 0.5 Checks, 0 g fat per heaped teaspoon. Serve with green vegetables or roasted peppers and tomatoes, which you can cook around the lamb.

Who would have thought of combining meat and fish? But don't turn up your nose at this curious combination – it works surprisingly well.

SERVES two 220 9 11 steak with red onion marmalade

Prep: **5** minutes   Cook: **20** minutes

A fabulous quick-fix for an extra-special supper. If wished, you can make the red onion marmalade in advance and store it for a few days in a screwtop jar in the fridge.

1 teaspoon olive oil
2 red onions, finely sliced
1 teaspoon sugar
1 teaspoon balsamic vinegar
2 x 150 g/5 oz fillet steaks
spray oil
salt and freshly ground black pepper
watercress, to garnish

1 Heat the olive oil in a pan and add the red onions. Cook them gently over a low heat for about 10–15 minutes, until softened and starting to caramelize. Stir in the sugar and balsamic vinegar and season to taste with salt and pepper. Cook gently for 5 more minutes.

2 Meanwhile, spray a ridged cast-iron grill pan with a little oil and place over a high heat. When it is really hot, place the fillet steaks in the pan and then grill for 3 minutes each side for rare; 4 minutes each side for medium rare; and 6–7 minutes each side for well done.

3 Arrange the cooked steaks on 2 warm serving plates, top with the red onion marmalade and serve, garnished with watercress sprigs. Lightly cooked spinach, seasoned with grated nutmeg, makes a good accompaniment.

OR...

You can cook the steaks under a conventional overhead grill. However, you will not get the delicious char-grilled flavour or attractive striped effect on the meat.

SERVES two 290 9 8 coriander and coconut spiced salmon

Prep: **10** minutes   Cook: **20** minutes

You may not have thought of combining an oily fish like salmon with spices, but they complement each other well. For the best flavour, if you can afford it, use organic or wild salmon.

1 garlic clove, crushed

1 small red chilli, de-seeded and finely chopped

juice of 1 lime

4 tablespoons finely chopped fresh coriander

4 tablespoons reduced-fat coconut milk

salt and freshly ground black pepper

2 x 150 g/5 oz salmon fillets, skinned

1 Mix together the garlic, chilli, lime juice, coriander and coconut milk, and season with salt and pepper. Alternatively, whizz in a blender until smooth.

2 Place the salmon fillets on a large sheet of foil in an ovenproof baking dish and spoon the spicy coconut mixture over them. Gather together the edges of the foil and make a parcel around the salmon.

3 Bake in a preheated oven at 200°C, 400°F, Gas Mark 6 for 15–20 minutes, until the salmon is cooked. Remove from the foil and serve hot with plenty of green vegetables.

SERVES two 250 10 9 roasted mediterranean cod

Prep: **5** minutes   Cook: **25** minutes

Cod is such a firm-fleshed succulent fish that it roasts really well – a much healthier cooking method than frying. Once you have prepared everything, which takes 5 minutes, you can just put it in the oven and forget about it. Nothing could be easier.

2 x 225 g/8 oz cod fillets, skinned and boned

3 tomatoes, halved

1 small red onion, quartered

1 green or yellow pepper, de-seeded and cut into chunks

1 small fennel bulb, cut into wedges

1 tablespoon capers

10 black olives

juice of 1 lemon

2 teaspoons olive oil

salt and freshly ground black pepper

2 tablespoons chopped parsley

1 Place the cod fillets, tomatoes, red onion, pepper and fennel in an ovenproof baking dish. Add the capers and olives and drizzle the lemon juice and olive oil over the top. Season with salt and plenty of freshly ground black pepper.

2 Cook in a preheated oven at 200°C, 400°F, Gas Mark 6 for about 25 minutes, until the cod is cooked through and the vegetables are tender.

3 Serve immediately, sprinkled with chopped parsley.

OR...

1 Other firm-fleshed white fish works equally well in this dish, especially monkfish tails or sea bass fillets.

2 You can vary the vegetables used by adding red peppers, courgettes or even potato wedges. If using potatoes, you must add 70 cals, 3 Checks, 0.5 g fat for each 100 g/3$\frac{1}{2}$ oz.

fish roll-ups with ratatouille

Prep: **10** minutes   Cook: **15** minutes

½ **red pepper, de-seeded and diced**

½ **yellow pepper, de-seeded and diced**

½ **small onion, finely chopped**

2 **large tomatoes, skinned and chopped**

5 **green olives, pitted and chopped**

spray oil

2 x 200 g/7 oz **lemon sole or plaice fillets, skinned**

1 **tablespoon red pesto sauce**

salt and freshly ground black pepper

1 Cook the red and yellow peppers, onion, tomatoes and olives for about 4–5 minutes in a hot pan that has been sprayed lightly with oil. The vegetables should be softened but not mushy and must still hold their shape.

2 Cut each fish fillet in half lengthways and then spread one side with the red pesto sauce. Bend each fillet round to form a hollow circle with the pesto side inwards, and secure with a wooden cocktail stick.

3 Place the fish rings on an ovenproof baking sheet and fill them with the cooked vegetable mixture. Season with a little salt and pepper.

4 Bake the filled fish fillet rings in a preheated oven at 200°C, 400°F, Gas Mark 6 for about 10 minutes, until the fish is cooked through and flakes easily. Transfer to warm serving plates and serve immediately with boiled green vegetables.

OR...

1 Spread 1 tablespoon tapenade or green pesto over the fish fillets instead of red pesto.

2 If you don't like ratatouille, never fear – you can make an alternative filling with a delicious mixture of steamed tender asparagus tips and baby carrots tossed in lemon juice. Cook as outlined above and serve topped with a spoonful of very low-fat fromage frais and some chopped herbs.

The finished dish looks and tastes so good that you could serve it when you are entertaining your family or friends. Any white fish fillets can be used.

thai spicy prawn curry

SERVES **two** 230 9 12

Prep: **10** minutes   Cook: **13** minutes

You can make this curry as hot as you like by varying the amount of chillies used. Or you can cheat and use some ready-made Thai curry paste, but this home-made mixture tastes fantastic and much more authentic.

2.5 cm/1 in piece fresh root ginger, peeled

1 stalk lemon grass, chopped

2 garlic cloves, crushed

2 spring onions, chopped

½ teaspoon ground cumin

½ teaspoon coriander seeds

small bunch fresh coriander

zest and juice of 1 lime

freshly ground black pepper

200 ml/7 floz reduced-fat coconut milk

1 teaspoon nam pla (Thai fish sauce)

115 g/4 oz fine green beans, trimmed and halved

2 kaffir lime leaves

225 g/8 oz peeled tiger prawns or cooked, peeled prawns

fresh basil leaves, to garnish

1 Put the ginger, lemon grass, garlic, spring onions, cumin, coriander seeds and leaves, lime zest and juice and plenty of black pepper in a blender or food processor, and whizz to a paste. If it seems too thick, you can add some more lime juice.

2 Put the coconut milk, nam pla, green beans and curry paste in a saucepan and simmer for about 10 minutes.

3 Add the prawns and continue simmering for 2–3 minutes, until they are thoroughly heated. If using raw tiger prawns, they will turn pink when cooked.

4 Serve the curry immediately, garnished with fresh basil. Thai fragrant rice is a good accompaniment to this dish but you will need to add 100 calories, 4 Checks, 0.5 g fat for each 75 g/2½ oz portion of boiled rice.

OR...

Create a vegetarian version by omitting the prawns and adding sliced green pepper, spring onions and asparagus with the beans. You will have 115 cals, 5 Checks and 11 g fat per serving.

SERVES two 220 9 13 potato and aubergine curry

Prep: **10** minutes   Cook: **20** minutes

This is much more inspirational than it sounds – a great curry in a hurry for veggies. If wished, you can grind your own spices instead of using a commercially prepared curry powder.

1 teaspoon vegetable oil
1 red onion, thinly sliced
1 aubergine, cut into chunks
225 g/8 oz potatoes, peeled and cubed
2 garlic cloves, crushed
2.5 cm/1 in piece fresh root ginger, peeled and finely chopped
1 red chilli, de-seeded and chopped
1 teaspoon ground cumin
1 teaspoon ground turmeric
1–2 teaspoons curry powder
200 ml/7 fl oz low-fat coconut milk
grated zest and juice of 1 lime
salt and black pepper
1 tablespoon chopped coriander

1 Heat the vegetable oil in a deep pan and add the red onion, aubergine and potatoes. Cook for about 5 minutes, turning occasionally, until softened.

2 Add the garlic, ginger, chilli, ground spices and curry powder, and cook for 2 minutes.

3 Add the coconut milk, and simmer gently for 10–15 minutes, until the potatoes are cooked. Add the lime zest and juice and season to taste. Serve, garnished with coriander.

OR...

Add colour to this spicy dish with some red peppers, thin green beans and quartered tomatoes.

SERVES two 415 17 17 quick garden vegetable lasagne

Prep: **10** minutes   Cook: **20** minutes

A traditional lasagne can be a very time-consuming, high-Check dish to make, but you can create a delicious vegetarian alternative in 30 minutes.

spray oil
1 red onion, chopped
2 garlic cloves, crushed
2 courgettes, thinly sliced
1 red or yellow pepper, de-seeded and chopped
1 x 200 g/7 oz can chopped tomatoes
salt and freshly ground black pepper
2 tablespoons chopped fresh basil or 1 teaspoon dried
6 lasagne sheets
225 g/8 oz ricotta cheese
2 teaspoons grated Parmesan cheese

1 Lightly spray a pan with oil and sauté the red onion, garlic, courgettes and peppers for 5 minutes. Add the canned tomatoes, seasoning and basil and cook for 5 minutes, until thickened.

2 Meanwhile, cook the lasagne in a large pan of boiling salted water for 10 minutes, until just tender. Drain well.

3 Spread half of the cooked vegetable mixture over the base of a baking dish. Cover with 3 sheets of lasagne and half the ricotta. Pour the remaining vegetable mixture over the top and cover with the rest of the lasagne sheets. Spread the remaining ricotta over the top and sprinkle with the Parmesan.

4 Bake in a preheated oven at 220°C, 425°F, Gas Mark 7 for 10 minutes. Serve hot with salad.

malaysian creamy spiced vegetables

SERVES **two** | **270** | **11** | **7**

Prep: **5** minutes   Cook: **25** minutes

1 teaspoon vegetable oil

2 medium potatoes, peeled and diced

1 onion, thinly sliced

225 g/8 oz chestnut mushrooms, quartered

1 teaspoon ground cumin

1 teaspoon ground turmeric

1 tablespoon garam masala

1 chilli, de-seeded and finely chopped

400 g/14 oz canned chopped tomatoes

250 ml/9 fl oz low-fat plain yogurt

salt and freshly ground black pepper

chopped fresh coriander, to garnish

1 Heat the oil in a deep pan and sauté the potatoes and onion for 5 minutes, until golden and softened. Add the mushrooms and cook for 2–3 minutes.

2 Stir in the cumin, turmeric, garam masala and chilli and cook for 1 minute.

3 Stir in the canned tomatoes and yogurt and cover the pan. Simmer very gently over a low heat for about 15 minutes, stirring occasionally, until the sauce is thick and creamy and the potatoes are cooked. Do not allow the mixture to boil, or it will curdle and separate.

4 Check the seasoning and serve hot, strewn with chopped coriander.

OR...

1 Add some aubergine with the potato, plus some crushed garlic and grated fresh ginger. Be adventurous with the fresh spices and have fun experimenting until you find the combination you like best.

2 If you really do want to omit the potato, serve this curry with some plain boiled rice. If so, allow 100 cals, 4 Checks, 0.5 g fat for each 30 g/1 oz dried weight or 75 g/2½ oz cooked weight portion.

3 Add 2 rounded tablespoons canned chick peas per serving and add 50 cals, 2 Checks, 1 g fat.

Although you can vary the vegetables in this economical dish, according to what you have available, the potatoes are essential. Serve with steamed green vegetables, such as mange tout, fine green beans or broccoli.

lemon scented asparagus risotto

Prep: **5** minutes   Cook: **20–25** minutes

225 g/8 oz asparagus spears, trimmed and cut into 1 cm (½ in) lengths

1 vegetable stock cube

spray oil

1 onion or 2 shallots, chopped

1 lemon grass stalk, finely chopped

175 g/6 oz risotto rice

sachet of powdered saffron

grated zest and juice of 1 lemon

salt and freshly ground black pepper

small bunch of mixed fresh herbs (parsley, chives, tarragon, etc.), chopped

2 tablespoons low-fat crème fraîche

1 Cook the asparagus in a pan of boiling salted water for about 6–8 minutes, until tender. Remove with a slotted spoon.

2 Crumble the vegetable stock cube into the cooking water and leave to simmer away gently.

3 While the asparagus is cooking, heat a large shallow pan which has been sprayed with oil. When hot, add the onion or shallots and the lemon grass, and cook for about 5 minutes, until softened but not brown.

4 Stir in the rice and cook for 1 minute before adding a ladleful of the hot vegetable stock and the saffron. Stir well and cook gently until absorbed, then add some more stock. Keep adding the stock in this way until the rice is tender and all the liquid has been absorbed.

5 Stir in the lemon zest and juice and the cooked asparagus and season to taste with salt and pepper.

6 Divide between 2 serving plates and serve scattered with chopped herbs and topped with the crème fraîche.

OR...

Instead of asparagus, you could use a selection of fresh vegetables, such as baby carrots, or shelled fresh peas and broad beans, in which case add 25 cals, 1 Check, 0 g fat per rounded tablespoon.

This is a lovely dish to make in late spring or early summer when asparagus is in season. For the best results, always use the proper risotto rice, such as arborio or carnaroli.

sweet

Even when you are slimming, you
can still enjoy a low-Check dessert.
In this chapter, you will find a range
of quick and easy recipes for some
delicious desserts that will not ruin
your weekly weight loss. Go on, treat
yourself – you deserve it!

Opposite: chocolate raspberry roulade (recipe on page 79)

SERVES **two** | **100** **4** ③ **affogate al caffe**

Prep: **5** minutes

This must be the quickest and easiest dessert imaginable – a seductive combination of sweet and bitter flavours. For the best results, do use real espresso coffee if you have a machine that makes this, but really strong black coffee will be OK.

2 small cups extremely hot, freshly made espresso coffee

4 x 60 ml scoops low-fat light vanilla ice cream

1 Make the coffee, using an espresso maker if you have one. It must be really strong and hot.

2 Scoop 2 neat balls of ice-cold vanilla ice cream into each of 2 bowls. The ice cream shoule be as frozen hard as possible so that it does not melt immediately the espresso is added.

3 Pour the espresso over and around the ice cream and serve and eat it at once – do not delay or the ice cream will melt into the coffee.

OR...

Instead of vanilla, you could use coffee ice cream. However, be careful to check the calorie count and fat content first, as some ice creams are way off the scale for slimmers.

oriental gingered fruit skewers

SERVES two | 200 8 0

Prep: **15** minutes   Cook: **6-8** minutes

Here's a novel way of serving fruit, and it's so easy to prepare and make. Perfect for a summer barbecue or even a bonfire party. You can buy star anise in the spice sections of most supermarkets and oriental stores.

60 ml/2 fl oz dry sherry
2 star anise
2.5 cm/1 in piece fresh root ginger, peeled and grated
pinch of five spice powder
2 level tablespoons caster sugar
1 small pineapple, peeled and cored
1 large mango, peeled and stoned

1 Put the sherry, star anise, ginger, five spice powder and sugar in a small saucepan. Place over a low heat and then stir gently until the sugar has completely dissolved. Turn up the heat and boil for 2–3 minutes until syrupy.

2 Cut the pineapple and mango into cubes and thread them on to 4 skewers. Place in a grill pan lined with foil and pour over the syrup.

3 Cook under a preheated hot grill for 6–8 minutes, turning them frequently and brushing with the syrup, until tender and slightly golden. Do not allow the fruit to become charred. Serve with very low-fat crème fraîche (50 cals, 2 Checks, 4 g fat per heaped tablespoon) or a scoop of low-calorie lemon sorbet (50 cals, 2 Checks, 0 g fat per 60 ml scoop).

passionfruit mini pavlovas

SERVES two | 75 3 0

Prep: **5** minutes

You can make the meringue bases yourself but it is time-consuming and will take ages to cook in a low oven. The cheat's way is to buy some ready-made meringue nests and then fill them with fresh fruit, making this the easiest dessert imaginable.

2 passionfruit
2 tablespoons Total 0% fat Greek yogurt
2 meringue nests
sprigs of fresh mint, to decorate

1 Cut the passionfruit in half and scoop out the seeds.

2 Mix with the Greek yogurt in a small bowl and spoon into the meringue nests.

3 Serve the pavlovas immediately, decorated with little sprigs of fresh mint leaves.

OR...

Mix the yogurt with sliced strawberries, raspberries, chopped peach or nectarine or ripe stoned cherries, depending on what fruit is in season and cheap and plentiful.

balsamic strawberries with mint

SERVES **two** | 125 **5** **0**

Prep: **10** minutes

225 g/8 oz ripe strawberries, hulled
2 tablespoons caster sugar
3 tablespoons good-quality balsamic vinegar
sprigs of mint, to decorate

Mint fromage frais:
150 g/5 oz very low-fat fromage frais
artificial sweetener, to taste (optional)
1–2 drops vanilla essence
1 tablespoon finely chopped fresh mint

1 You can leave the strawberries whole or cut them in half if they are quite large. Place them in a bowl and sprinkle with the caster sugar. Drizzle the balsamic vinegar over the top and set aside to marinate for at least 20 minutes.

2 If wished, sweeten the fromage frais to taste and stir in the vanilla essence and chopped mint.

3 Serve the strawberries in their marinade with the mint fromage frais.

A novel way of serving strawberries, you can make this dessert in advance and leave it to marinate for an hour or so. You must use balsamic vinegar – malt or wine vinegars will not work!

tiramisu

SERVES **two** | 230 **9** **4**

Prep: **15** minutes

1 egg yolk
1 tablespoon caster sugar
1–2 drops vanilla essence
175 g/6 oz skimmed milk Quark
50 ml/2 fl oz hot strong coffee
1 teaspoon brandy
6 sponge fingers
1 level teaspoon cocoa powder

1 In a bowl, beat the egg yolk and sugar with a wooden spoon until thick and creamy. Stir in the vanilla essence and beat in the Quark.

2 Pour the hot coffee into a small bowl and stir in the brandy. Dip 3 of the sponge fingers into this and place them in the bottom of 2 small glass dishes or sundae glasses. Cover with half of the creamy Quark mixture.

3 Dip the remaining sponge fingers into the hot coffee and arrange them on top of the Quark. Spoon the rest of the Quark on top, smooth level and then dust lightly with cocoa powder. Chill in the refrigerator until required.

Everyone loves this Sicilian dessert but you've never tasted a low-fat version like this before. For the best flavour, use very strong espresso coffee. This recipe contains raw egg so it is not suitable for babies, young children, pregnant women, the elderly or anyone with a compromised immune system.

pancakes with spiced apple filling

SERVES four | 200 | 8 | 1

Prep: **5** minutes Cook: **15** minutes

Pancakes are so easy to cook and everybody always loves them. These make a pleasant change from the usual lemon and sugar ones for which the calorie, Check and fat gram counts are given below.

125 g/4½ oz plain flour
pinch of salt
1 large egg
300 ml/½ pint skimmed milk
spray oil
fine strips of lemon zest to decorate

Spiced apple filling:
2 cooking apples, peeled, cored and cut into chunks
artificial sweetener, to taste
pinch of cinnamon
grated zest and juice of ½ lemon

1 Sift the flour and salt into a large bowl, and then beat in the egg and skimmed milk until you have a really smooth batter. Alternatively, use a blender or food processor for this.

2 Cook the apple with a little water in a heavy based pan over a medium heat until the apple is softened. Add artificial sweetener to taste together with a pinch of cinnamon and the lemon zest and juice.

3 Heat a small frying pan and, when it is hot, spray lightly with oil. Add a little of the batter, tilting the pan and swirling it around so that it covers the base.

4 Cook over a medium heat until it is golden and set underneath, then flip it over and cook the other side. Slide the pancake out onto a serving plate and then keep warm while you cook the remaining pancakes.

5 Put a little of the apple filling on each pancake and roll up or fold over. Serve hot sprinkled with lemon zest. Sprinkle a little more lemon juice over if wished.

OR...

You could save time by just opting for the traditional lemon pancakes. Omit the filling – just squeeze some fresh lemon juice over the pancakes, sprinkle with sweetener and roll up (160 cals, 6 Checks, 1 g fat per 2 unfilled pancakes).

SERVES two | 140 6 0 rhubarb and ginger fruit fool

Prep: **5** minutes   Cook: **10** minutes

Fools are very old British desserts. The name probably comes from the French word fouler, meaning 'to crush'. Usually made with mounds of whipped cream, our low-Check version uses 0% fat Greek yogurt.

- **350 g/12 oz tender pink rhubarb**
- **30 g/1 oz caster sugar**
- **2 knobs preserved stem ginger in syrup, drained and chopped**
- **1 tablespoon ginger syrup**
- **1 tablespoon orange juice**
- **150 g/5 oz Total 0% fat Greek yogurt**

1 Trim the ends of the rhubarb and cut the stems into chunks. Place in a pan with the sugar, preserved ginger, ginger syrup and orange juice.

2 Place the pan over a very low heat and then cook at a bare simmer for about 8–10 minutes, turning occasionally, until the rhubarb is really tender and cooked. Remove from the pan and allow to cool slightly.

3 In a serving bowl, gently swirl the cooked rhubarb mixture into the yogurt until it is well blended and attractively streaked with pink. Serve chilled.

SERVES two | 150 6 0 cheat's fruit brûlée

Prep: **5** minutes   Cook: **5** minutes

A traditional crème brûlée is made with full-fat cream and is high in calories and fat grams. This quick and easy version is lighter, healthier and far less cloying. It will make a refreshing end to a slimming meal.

- **115 g/4 oz fresh raspberries**
- **115 g/4 oz fresh strawberries, hulled**
- **150 g/5 oz Total 0% fat Greek yogurt**
- **2 heaped tablespoons demerara sugar**

1 Divide the raspberries and strawberries between 2 heatproof ramekin dishes.

2 Spoon the yogurt over the fruit to completely cover it and place in the fridge for 5 minutes to keep cold.

3 Heat the grill until it is really hot – on its highest setting. Sprinkle the sugar lightly over the yogurt to cover it and then pop under the hot grill until the sugar caramelizes and turns evenly golden. Watch it carefully to prevent it burning.

4 Remove the ramekins and allow to cool before returning them to the refrigerator until you are ready for them. Don't dig in while the caramel is still hot, or you will burn your mouth!

chocolate raspberry roulade

SERVES six | 130 5 4

Prep: **15** minutes   Cook: **10** minutes

3 eggs
60 g/2 oz caster sugar
85 g/3 oz self-raising flour
3 rounded teaspoons unsweetened cocoa powder
150 ml/¼ pint very low-fat raspberry fromage frais
115 g/4 oz fresh raspberries
icing sugar for dusting

1 Line a Swiss roll tin with non-stick parchment paper.

2 In a clean, dry bowl, whisk the eggs and caster sugar until the mixture is pale and light in texture.

3 Sift in the flour and cocoa powder, and gently fold in with a metal spoon in a figure-of-eight movement.

4 Pour the mixture into the prepared tin and spread out with a palette knife to cover the whole surface.

5 Bake in a preheated oven at 200°C, 400°F, Gas Mark 6 for 8–10 minutes, until the sponge is firm and springy to the touch.

6 Turn out the sponge onto a large sheet of greaseproof paper, then peel away the lining paper. Trim the edges, cover with a clean, damp tea towel and set aside for a few minutes to cool.

7 Spread the fromage frais over the sponge and scatter with the raspberries. Roll up carefully and transfer to a serving plate with the long edge underneath the roulade. Dust with icing sugar and serve, cut into slices.

Don't be put off by the name of this recipe; it's much easier to make than it sounds and it does not take long either. Instead of calorie-laden whipped cream, it is filled with very low-fat raspberry fromage frais.

fruity amaretti layers

SERVES two | 160 6 1

Prep: **15** minutes

1 small ripe mango
1 x 200 g/7 oz pot natural low-fat fromage frais
60 g/2 oz raspberries
4 amaretti biscuits, crushed

1 Slice the mango down either side of the long stone. Remove the skin and cut the flesh into dice. Use all the mango in this way.

2 Place the mango in 2 small glass dishes or sundae glasses. Cover with half the fromage frais.

3 Whizz the raspberries to a purée in a blender or push through a sieve. Spoon the purée over the fromage frais and cover with most of the crushed amaretti biscuits.

4 Top with the remaining fromage frais and sprinkle with the rest of the amaretti before serving chilled.

Slightly bitter and intensely almondy, amaretti complement the sweetness of the mango. If you have a very sweet tooth, you can add some artificial sweetener to the fromage frais.

Index